The American Revolutionary Series

THE LOYALIST LIBRARY

The American Revolutionary Series
is published in cooperation with
The Boston Public Library

The Delaware Loyalists

By
HAROLD BELL HANCOCK

With a New Introduction and Preface by
GEORGE ATHAN BILLIAS

GREGG PRESS
Boston 1972

Library of Congress Cataloging in Publication Data

Hancock, Harold Bell, 1913-
    The Delaware loyalists.

    (American Revolutionary series)
    Reprint of the 1940 ed.
    1. American loyalists—Delaware. 2. Delaware—
History—Revolution. I. Title. II. Series.
E277.H25   1972   973.3'14   72-8730
ISBN 0-8398-0800-3

THE LOYALIST LIBRARY

THE LOYALISTS in the American Revolution represent one of the most misunderstood groups in our nation's history. For the past two centuries, they have fared badly at the hands of historians; Tories have either been neglected, or protrayed in an unsympathetic light by ultra-patriotic writers. The remark that a Loyalist was "a thing whose head is in England . . . body . . . in America, and its neck ought to be stretched," typifies the common attitude during the first century after the Revolution. This early period was one of outspoken nationalism, and resentment against the Loyalists and former mother country remained high. Although Anglo-American animosities diminished in the second century, and scholars adopted a more detached approach, the Tories were studied only sporadically. The present collection—called the Loyalist Library—contains both writings of important Tories and scholarly monographs on the subject. It should help to stimulate renewed research and interest in this forgotten part of America's past.

History is usually written by winners, not losers, and therefore we do not know as much about the Loyalists as we should. For one thing, we do not know how many Tories there actually were. The old estimate—mistakenly attributed to John Adams—claimed that the country was split three ways during the war: one-third becoming

Loyalists; one-third supporting the patriot cause; and one-third remaining neutral or indifferent. Modern scholars estimate that the Tories comprised something closer to nineteen percent of the total number of white Americans. Several studies included in this collection, such as Otis G. Hammond's *Tories of New Hampshire,* and Janet B. Johnson's biography of Robert Alexander, a Maryland Loyalist, provide evidence that casts serious doubts on the older assumption.

The Loyalist Library should help to correct another misconception—the idea that Tories came mainly from the upper class—from the ranks of royal officeholders, rich merchants, professional men, and well-to-do Anglicans. Recent research into the socio-economic background of Tories reveals that they hailed instead from the middle or lower classes in most of the colonies. Farmers, artisans, and small businessmen formed the backbone of the Loyalist movement for the most part. Wilbur H. Siebert's work on *The Loyalists of Pennsylvania,* for example, shows that in the Quaker colony many frontier farmers became Tories.

In geographical terms, the Loyalists were scattered throughout all of the original thirteen colonies. Virginia and Massachusetts had the smallest number. The strongest Tory support seems to have been in certain of the Middle Colonies—New York, New Jersey, and Pennsylvania—and in the South—in the Carolinas and Georgia. State studies of these areas, such as Edward Alfred Jones' *The Loyalists of New Jersey* and Harold B. Hancock's *The Delaware Loyalists,* tell us specifically who the Tories were—their names, place of residence, occupation or profession, and religion. Loyalists, moreover, tended to concentrate in urban areas and along the seacoast—except in New York, North Carolina, and parts of Pennsylvania where major pockets of Tories could be found in the interior. The treatment that Tories received at the hands of the Whigs in such seacoast cities as Boston may be gleaned from Arthur W. Eaton's biography of Mather Byles.

The Loyalist Library also provides proof that the Floridas and Nova Scotia—none of which rebelled—may have held the highest ratio of Tories. Wilbur H. Siebert's *Loyalists in East Florida, 1774 to 1785* indicates that the number of Tories in that colony increased substantially as a result of the exodus from the Carolinas and Georgia. The papers of Edward Winslow reflect the problems that incoming Loyalists encountered in resettling in Nova Scotia.

It is estimated that seventy-five to eighty thousand Loyalists left the United States during the war for England, Canada, the West Indies, and other parts of the British empire. Pamphlets of refugees like Joseph Galloway, which are reprinted here, reveal much about the views of the Loyalists who went to England. Some individuals remained men without a country, and lived out their days in London while dreaming about America. Others took up careers on the continent, as is evident in George E. Ellis' *Memoir of Sir Benjamin Thompson, Count Rumford.* Another major group—the United Empire Loyalists—whose story is presented in certain of these writings, settled in Canada and became the founding fathers of new communities.

The Loyalist Library includes also valuable primary source materials. Loyalist letters, pamphlets, and personal narratives help to shed light on the key question: Why did the American Tories remain loyal to their King? Prominent Loyalists like Daniel Leonard of Massachusetts and Joseph Galloway of Pennsylvania explain their political position in their writings. They tell us what they considered to be the proper relationship between colonies and mother country, the King and his subjects, and colonial governors and the American people. Until we view the Loyalists as men with "positive political ideas" and individuals capable of "creative statesmanship," a balanced interpretation of the Revolution will elude us, says one historian.

The Loyalist Library, then, is a combination of primary source documents and secondary materials. It includes private letters, diaries, and narratives, Tory histories and pamphlets, as well as scholarly books written on the subject. The collection makes available certain sources that were heretofore less accessible, and it should enable students to become more familiar with the Loyalist side of the story of the Revolution.

PREFACE

DELAWARE, smallest of the original thirteen
colonies, appears to have had a large number of Loyalists.
Contemporaries on both sides—John Adams and Joseph
Galloway—agreed that the Loyalists may have been in the
majority, or at the very least made a strong showing.
Certain subsequent historians, however, took a contrary
point of view. They claimed that the colony contained
fewer Loyalists than any other south of New England,
except for Virginia.

Professor Harold B. Hancock, the leading scholar of
Delaware Loyalists, takes issue with the latter position. He
estimates that about fifty percent of the inhabitants were
Loyalists, thirty percent patriots, and twenty percent
pacifists or hesitant in taking sides. The weight of the
evidence appears to support Hancock, who marshals an
impressive array of data in this study.

Hancock explains the large number of Delaware Loyalists
partly on social and geographical grounds. The majority of
Delaware's inhabitants, he argues, were small farmers who
were contented with their lot. They lived in rather isolated
areas which had few roads, newspapers, or schools. The
result, he concluded, was the development of an innate
conservatism.

Religion likewise played an important role in determining
the political persuasion of those involved in the Revolution.

The second strongest denomination in the colony were the Anglicans, many of whom became Loyalists. By contrast the colony's strongest religious sect were the Presbyterians, who mainly supported the patriot cause.

Hancock's book contains interesting sociological data. His list of "Loyalists Excepted From Pardon By the Act of June 26, 1778," for example, identifies these persons in terms of their occupation as well as place of residence.

The Hancock work remains the best in-depth study we have of the Delaware Loyalists.

George Athan Billias
Clark University

THE
DELAWARE
LOYALISTS

THE
DELAWARE
LOYALISTS

By
HAROLD BELL HANCOCK

❧

HISTORICAL SOCIETY OF DELAWARE
Wilmington, Delaware
1940

Papers of
The Historical Society of Delaware
New Series, No. III

Printed By:
HAMBLETON PRINTING and PUBLISHING COMPANY
Wilmington, Delaware

To
MY PARENTS

Contents

Preface

*A*mong the neglected subjects in Delaware history is the story of the loyalists. With the exception of Delaware such a study has been completed for the other original colonies. The disagreement in Delaware between contemporary writers and present-day historians gives the topic unusual interest. It is the purpose of this paper to examine in detail the activities of the loyalists and to arrive at some conclusions.

Newspapers or manuscripts were consulted at the following institutions: Library of Congress, University of Virginia, Maryland Historical Society, Pennsylvania Historical Society, Philadelphia Library Company, New York Public Library, American Antiquarian Society, Massachusetts Historical Society, Widener Library, Wilmington Library, Delaware State Archives, University of Delaware Library, and Historical Society of Delaware. Manuscript material of special importance is found in the court records at Dover, in the transcripts of British records in the New York Public Library, and in the Delaware papers in the Library of Congress. Valuable printed sources are *Letters to and from Caesar Rodney,* edited by Dr. George H. Ryden, the third volume of the *Delaware Archives,* and the proceedings of the Assembly and Council. Newspapers in Pennsylvania paid scant attention to developments within the borders of its tiny neighbor. For the most part secondary accounts are unimportant, but an exception is the excellent monograph by Henry Clay Reed on "The Delaware Constitution of 1776."

With pleasure I acknowledge aid and encouragement from several persons. Dr. George H. Ryden and Mr. Henry Clay Reed, of the University of Delaware, gave the paper the benefit of a careful reading. Mr. Leon deValinger patiently and kindly guided my exploration of the materials assembled at the Archives Office. It is through the interest of Mr. Christopher L. Ward, President of the Delaware Historical Society, and the generosity of its official Board and members that the paper is published.

HAROLD BELL HANCOCK.

August 15, 1940,
Dover, Delaware.

THE
DELAWARE
LOYALISTS

THE
DELAWARE
LOYALISTS

CHAPTER I.

The Setting for the Revolution

THE DISAGREEMENT OVER THE NUMBER
OF LOYALISTS

WRITERS on Delaware history frequently give the impression that the residents of the state were as loyal to American independence as Colonel Haslet's regiment. "The proportion of the disaffected to the total population," wrote an exponent of this view in an article upon "Cheney Clow's Rebellion," "was probably smaller in Delaware than in any other colony south of New England except Virginia. The population of the 'Three Lower Counties' in 1766 was about 37,000. Of these perhaps 10,000 were either lukewarm or actively in opposition to war measures."[1] Judge Conrad estimated that the soldiers supplied to the Continental Army by Delaware more than equalled in number all the males within the State aged 16 to 44, and thus he implies that the majority of the inhabitants were revolutionists.[2] Did he know that it was a common practice to send troublesome Tories who participated in insurrections off to serve in the American Army?[3] An examination of the statements of Whig, Tory, and British observers, however, will reveal quite a different picture. John Adams in 1780 considered that there were "in this little State, from various causes, more tories in proportion, than in any other."[4] Thomas McKean years after the Revolution declared, "A majority of the State was against the independence."[5] An examination of the correspondence of Caesar Rodney confirms

1

these opinions.[6]   Joseph Galloway, one of America's most distinguished Tories, said, "There was throughout the War a Majority in favor of retaining their Allegiance."[7]   British officers were well-pleased with the attitude of the inhabitants.   "The People in the Counties upon the Delaware, upon the Coast of which I am writing," observed a lieutenant on board a British vessel off the shore from New Castle in October, 1777, "are certainly well-affected in general, and have brought us large supplies of everything we wanted."[8]   After the defeat at Yorktown, Lord George Germain recommended the establishment of a post in the lower counties of Delaware, "as they are from their situation easily defended, have in them plenty of provision for the subsistence of an army, and the inhabitants in general wish to return to their allegiance."[9] Contemporaries, then, state definitely that Delaware was a loyalist province, though some historians give credence to the idea that most Delawareans backed the Continental Congress.

Probably both judgments require revision.   While participants in the Revolution swelled the number of loyalists by inclusion of an important and distinct third class, hesitants and pacifists like the Quakers, present-day writers underestimate the strength of the disaffected.   Delaware may be justly proud of the fame of its Blue Hen Chicken troops, but it should not forget the other side of the Revolution, for which so many of its inhabitants sacrificed property, country, and life.

THE CONDITION OF DELAWARE IN 1775

A great contrast between past and present appears when one examines the condition of society in Delaware 160 years ago. Radical changes have occurred in the interval in the size of population and racial composition, in government and industry, in transportation and communication.   At the beginning of the Revolution the three counties on the Delaware possessed a population of 37,219, including 2,000 slaves and many bonded servants. New Castle contained 14,295 inhabitants; Kent, 8,996; Sussex, 13,928.[10]   The majority of Delawareans were descended from English stock, but the Scotch-Irish formed a sizeable minority.[11] Thomas McKean even maintained that they dominated racially in New Castle County.[12]   Perhaps this statement is exaggerated.   But the Pennsylvania newspapers of the period printed frequent notices of Scotch-Irish apprentices who had run away from masters in New Castle County, and the Presbyterian Church, to which this group largely belonged, claimed more adherents by far in the vicinity than any other sect.[13]   The strength of the Presbyterians and Scotch-Irish, as McKean asserted,[14] was a major factor in explaining the staunch patriotism of New Castle County.   By 1766 the Presbyterians had established 29 churches.   Next in number and influence came the Episcopalians and Quakers, each of whom maintained 12 churches; these two denominations were influential in the southern part of the State.[15]

Although Delaware and Pennsylvania still retained the same governor, the three lower counties with their own unicameral legislature and laws had been practically independent since 1702. Riotous elections returned such leaders as Caesar Rodney, George Read, and John Dickinson to prominent places in the government. Not even the effective preaching of Charles Inglis in the sixties could more than temporarily stay the "scenes of debauchery and vice" which took place annually on such occasions in Kent County.[16]   The principal occupation was farming; grain found a ready market in the numerous flour mills along the Brandywine.[17] Then as now, Wilmington was the metropolis; with 2,000 inhabitants,[18] it had merit enough to be called, "a well built, commodious, and populous town" by a contemporary observer.[19]   Of even smaller size and significance were Newark, New Castle, Duck Creek Crossroads (Smyrna), Dover, and Lewes.   As missionaries and stray travelers have recorded, journeys through swamps and over roads filled with mud-holes were difficult;[20] quicker and easier transportation might be obtained on the sloops which sailed the winding, shallow creeks and Bay.   Schools were few and inferior, with the birch rod used as a common stimulant to learning.[21]   Because Delaware had no newspapers, residents naturally regarded Philadelphia as their journalistic center.

Perhaps the Diamond State seems to have been unduly backward, judged by modern standards, but relatively, compared to the South, its condition was superior.   A French traveler in 1782 with the agreeable habit of praising everything American found Delaware an extremely pleasant place.   He especially commended Dover for its elegant appearance and neatness.   "All the Americans whom we met," he observed during his stay at the present-day capital, "were dressed in well-made clothes of excellent stuff, with boots well-cleaned;—their deportment was free, frank, and kind, equally removed from rudeness of manner and from studied politeness. . . ."[22] Delawareans were not bashful in praising the virtues of their State. For a Philadelphia magazine in 1789, Dr. James Tilton wrote a glowing account of Delaware's agricultural resources in the rose-colored style characteristic of the pamphlets distributed by the Board of Agriculture today. "The inhabitants of this state," he claimed, "are generally tall, muscular, active, and remarkably enterprising. The Delaware regiment was notoriously one of the finest and most efficient in the continental army."[23] An acute observer at the beginning of the Revolution might have predicted the loyalist and patriot sections of Delaware. Just as New Castle County with its bustling commercial life, its numerous travelers, and its Scotch-Irish, Presbyterian population developed into a hot-bed of patriotism, lower Delaware with its backward, rural population, its strong Episcopalian Church, and its isolation emerged the stronghold of the loyalists. Different environments bred different sentiments.

In the troublesome decade before the Revolution, the three counties on the Delaware had supported the steps taken to preserve liberty.[24] The maltreatment of the district stamp-collector in 1765 had been approved, and two delegates attended the Stamp Act Convention in New York. As in the other colonies, a non-importation agreement was enforced; great rejoicing occurred at the repeal of the hateful measure, and an address of thankfulness was moved to the throne. But Great Britain had not finished coercing her over-seas dependencies, for two years later came the Townshend acts. Under pressure from Philadelphia merchants, a new non-importation agreement was finally adopted in New Castle County in August, 1769. Again Great Britain repented her severity, though the duty on tea was retained. In 1773 the East India Company began the wholesale importation of the commodity into the country. "The Committee for tarring and feathering" immediately threatened punishment to the person sailing the ill-ladened craft up the Delaware River; "like *Cain,* he will be hung out as the *damned traitorous pilot who brought up the tea-ship."* Under threats of violence at Chester the ship was compelled to return to England without landing its cargo.[25]

After the passage of the Boston Port Act in 1774, the unfortunate residents of the Massachusetts capital found abundant sympathy in Delaware. Meetings were held in New Castle, Dover, and Lewes, and committees, among whose members were some later loyalists,[26] collected several hundred pounds in relief money.

Caesar Rodney, Thomas McKean, and George Read represented Delaware at the first meeting of the Continental Congress; this body adopted an address of remonstrance to the King and an act which practically prohibited the importation of British goods. War appeared more than an idle threat by the end of 1774, when militia companies were already being formed in the northern part of the State. So far the three counties on the Delaware had done their share in resisting odious Parliamentary measures. But in the succeeding year, as the struggle progressed in seriousness and severity—with the shot heard around the world, with the raising of the Continental Army, and no signs of weakening evident on the side of Great Britain—strong-arm methods became necessary to assure the co-operation of all the inhabitants.

THE GROWING DIVISION BETWEEN
WHIG AND TORY

In 1775 Tory and Whig were the names of political parties in Delaware. The demarcation between these factions, as a distinction between loyalist and patriot, developed during the War. While it is practically impossible to fix the exact date for the shift of opinion, Allen McLane many years after the Revolution, argued that the occasion was June, 1776, when a petition for the establishment of a new government was being circulated, which both sides realized "savoured" of independence. "At this time," wrote McLane, "the line was drawn between Whig and Tory. those opposed to Independence was Demonated [sic] Torys and many of the Whigs treated them as Enemies. When the Question was first Agitated in the committees a Considerable Majority was Opposed to the measure. the few whigs (and very few indeed), became Desperate Dreaded the Consequence of being Captured and treated as Rebels. Attacked the Disaffected with Tar and Feathers, Rotten Eggs &c &c. and succeeded in silencing the Disaffected and then filling these Committees with men Determined to be free."[27] Timoleon confirms this account of how Delaware took the first steps towards independence.[28] As early as May 1, 1776, Caesar Rodney had commented concerning an election in Philadelphia: "The Terms for the parties are Whig & Tory— dependance & Independence—."[29]

Although Whig and Tory still signified political parties after the spring of 1776, the latter eventually became thoroughly discredited as the party of rebellion. To a good Whig, a Tory came to mean a person whose head is in Great Britain, whose body is in America, and whose neck ought to be stretched.[30] In reality, the Tories were not the murderous, scheming plotters described by the Whigs, but men with honest differences of opinion. Many Tories had gladly supported peaceful measures against Great Britain, but they refused to consider actual independence and war; for this stand they were condemned by the Whigs as traitors. The Whigs insisted that everyone take sides, preferably on the side of independence. Joshua Hill, a wealthy loyalist exiled from Sussex County, has left a vivid, laconic narrative of how he became the vilest of creatures in the eyes of the Whigs: Having taken "part with the British Government when Troubles broke out, [he] refused to take part with Americans, therefore they said as he was not with them, he was against them, [he] was ill used & Abused, had Oath of Allegiance offered, but refused, was carried before their Committees but refused." Finally, he was driven from his home in March, 1778, when a plundering band of Whigs threatened his very life.[31] After independence had been declared, some Tories turned Whig, some tried to remain neutral, while others showed their devotion to the mother country by attempting to reestablish the old order. Even before the great moment to decide came in July, 1776, many residents had already demonstrated their displeasure at the violent methods recommended by the Continental Congress to heal the breach.

Perhaps it is significant that relatively few instances of resistance have been preserved for New Castle County. The first case concerned the famous Baptist minister and historian, Rev. Morgan Edwards. At Newark in August, 1775, he confessed his regret at the "use of rash and imprudent expressions with respect to the conduct of my fellow-countrymen, who are now engaged in a noble and patriotick struggle for the liberties of America against the arbitrary measures of the British ministry."[32] Hugh Calhoon, of St. George's Hundred, in the same month uttered a similar retraction; in the future he promised to support resistance.[33] Under the terms of the non-exportation act, an Irish ship at Wilmington in September was refused permission to load freight.[34]

Vigorous steps in defense of American liberty were undertaken in Kent County. The first person to feel the wrath of the local committee was a mysterious J. H., who attempted to import an inordinate amount of tea in barrels from Jamaica; until instructions were received from Philadelphia, the goods were stored in a ware-house.[35] A letter in the *Pennsylvania Ledger* on February 7 asserted that residents of Kent County still loved King George and that on second thought they repented seeing fiery addresses sent to His Majesty by the Continental Congress. The writer believed that "if the King's standard were now erected, nine out of ten would repair to it."[36] Naturally, the Dover organization denied the accusation. Had not the inhabitants of the county assumed "a virtuous stand against tyranny and oppression"? Obviously, such a note was designed only to cause division and excite distrust.[37] When investigation disclosed that Robert Holliday, a Quaker,[38] had composed the "base calumny, replete with false-hood," two letters of confession of error were required to settle the matter to the satisfaction of the committee.[39] A group of Whigs in March had some fun with a resigned tax-collector named Byrnes, who had audaciously seized two wagons near Duck Creek Cross-roads, "for reasons best known to himself," and was endeavoring to drive them out of the State. After wrecking his gun and giving him a drink of "Newberry rum" taken from a duck-hole, the pranksters forced him to "damn Bute, North, and their brethren for a parcel of Ministerial Sons of Bitches." Finally, he was "varnished and feathered" before being expelled from the colony to express these sentiments in Boston and Europe.[40] Whigs and Tories could play the same games. Joseph Parsons sorrowfully informed the committee in July that he had been tarred and feathered by some residents of Murderkill Hundred, "for no other reason, than *that he was a Constable*"; they also had declared, "That they should pay no longer any obedience to the Civil Authority;—for that there was no King, nor any Law since the passing [of] the Quebec Act." Alarmed by the outbreaks of a licentious spirit in the district, the committee unanimously recommended obedience to the existing form of government.[41]

As the Rev. Mr. Sydenham Thorn of the Anglican Church refused to observe July 20 as a day of humiliation and prayer despite the recommendation of Congress and encouraged many to submit "to the Arbitrary Attempts of the Ministry and Parliament to enslave America," he was brought before the Committee of Correspondence in September, though the action taken is unknown.[42] Dr. Charles Ridgely, of Dover, told Daniel Mifflin in July, 1775, "that he allowed we could not defend ourselves against the Powers of England." When it was suggested that the members of Congress were sensible men, he replied, "They Might be, but he did not think they acted like sensible Men." Holliday's letter in February, he believed, had done much good. Brought before the Committee at its September meeting, he was acquitted, although many continued to regard him as "the Ring-leader of all the Toryism of this State," and talk of tarring and feathering him circulated.[43] A month later Daniel Varnum expressed regret for various unpatriotic utterances. In conversation with a friend he had maintained that "he had as lief be under a tyrannical King as a tyrannical Commonwealth, especially if the d——d Presbyterians had the control of it.[44] Another case concerning a Quaker came before the Kent County committee in January, 1776. For refusing to accept Continental paper money on religious grounds, John Cowgill, of Duck Creek, was denounced as an enemy to this country; millers refused to grind his corn, and the schoolmaster sent his children home. On one occasion he was stopped by a group of armed men, who fastened a sign on his back with the inscription, "On the Circulation of the Continental Currency depends the fate of America," and paraded through the streets of Dover in a cart amidst great excitement.[45]

While a committee of public safety was not established in Sussex County until June 20, 1775, it soon became engaged in a deadlock match with its most influential inhabitant. The committee explained its delay in organizing by the long-winded boundary dispute with Maryland, "and not from the influence of any Tories amongst us, or any disregard to the common cause." After the government of "New Sussex," a new county in southwestern Delaware, was set up, it hoped to raise 1500 militia.[46] In November, Samuel McMasters wrote to Dr. James Tilton that the Grand Jury had indicted some men for rioting against a certain J. C. Two months earlier, J. C. had cursed Congress at Lewes and stated that "the d——d set would ruin the country." When the committee took up his case, he remained defiant, but the new mode of making converts—tarring and feathering—had been rejected. Although only a drum had been beaten and two eggs thrown, the King's attorney had successfully prosecuted an indictment against them.[47] Tilton in reply recommended energetic measures against such enemies of liberty, for the law of nature justified a rash course. During the present crisis he could not understand the attitude of the deluded jurors who had returned the indictment; anywhere else in the colonies Tories would receive proper instruction and suitable correction.[48] Dr. Tilton also expressed his displeasure in a similar vein to one of the jurors; he hoped that the indictments would be quashed.[49]

With some qualms the Sussex County committee approached the case of Thomas Robinson—rich, powerful, and defiant legislator—who exercised much control over the inhabitants in the section by his office and store. But his open and bold attempts "to stamp his vile and slavish Ministerial principles upon the weak and unwary" in the forests of Sussex County and the nearby parts of Maryland demanded a reprimand. Witnesses testified that he had sold tea, called Congress an "unconstitutional body of men," and stated that the poor were "a pack of fools" to arm against the King, since their leaders would later desert them. After denouncing him as "an enemy to his Country and a contumacious opposer to liberty," the committee recommended boycotting. Without being accompanied by forty or fifty companions, Robinson refused to appear before the body to answer the charges.[50] In a letter to the *Pennsylvania Journal* in October he complained that the committee had exceeded its powers, for only a few members had signed the resolutions.[51] He produced a statement from five of its members, who declared the charges to be "without foundation."[52] The question of Robinson's patriotism flared up again in March, 1776, when on the way to a meeting of the Assembly, he was jailed by some militia officers at Dover until his conduct could be investigated. After his colleague, Colonel Jacob Moore, intervened with a sword and demonstrated a willingness to defend Robinson's life at the risk of his own, he also was held.[53] The Kent County delegation urged their release because of urgent business.[54] Upon expressing regret for their imprudent actions and agreeing to allow the legislature to determine their fitness for a seat in that august body, they were permitted to proceed to New Castle. A resolution signed by the militia officers at Dover specifically exempted Thomas Rodney from ordering their seizure.[56] Timoleon gives George Read, "tyrant of Delaware," the credit for the failure to prosecute.[57]

The Rev. Philip Reading, pastor of an Episcopalian Church at Appoquinimink, has left an excellent account of the difficult domestic situation in Delaware in the spring of 1776 in a report to the Society for the Propagation of the Gospel. As early as March, 1775, he had claimed: "Many are the rebuffs I am obliged to encounter on the subject of the present commotions, notwithstanding which I am not deterred or discouraged from inculcating the principles of Loyalty to our most gracious Sovereign and a due submission to the Powers of Government on all proper occasions."[58] A year later he asserted that it was almost impossible to remain neutral in the struggle between Great Britain and her colonies. "Much industry," he wrote, "has been used to render me obnoxious to the popular resentment as being inimical to the measures prosecuting here in opposition to the Parliamentary authority of the present state. *No more passive obedience and non resistance* has been scribbled with a pencil on my Church door. It was urged as a just cause of complaint against one of the Captains of the Militia that he had lugged his company to Church on the day of a public fast *to hear that old wretch* (meaning myself) *preach, who was always an enemy to the present measures."* Thus far he had persisted in mentioning the King in his public prayers. A previous letter containing the above sentiment had been confiscated by a committtee of inspection in Philadelphia, but had not been thought worthy of censure.[59] On July 28, 1776, however, he had to close his church for six weeks, since he "could not read the Liturgy agreeably to the prescribed form without offending against our Government and incurring the resentment of the people."[60] Apparently, his charge was not reopened during the Revolution.

These instances demonstrate conclusively that independence was advocated only by radicals in Delaware in 1775 and the spring of 1776. While numerous Tories were compelled to express approval of the measures adopted by the Continental Congress, not one was asked to sanction complete separation. The principal object of the committees of inspection was to secure co-operation in resistance; such unity alone might achieve the aims of the colonists legally. The idea of independence came to many Delawareans as a disagreeable shock in June, 1776.

CHAPTER II.

The Revolution and the Tories in the Early Years

DISAFFECTION PRIOR TO JULY 4, 1776

MEANWHILE, steps for the defense of the province had been undertaken. Pennsylvania employed Henry Fisher as a lookout scout for its Council of Safety at Lewes and strung a chevaux-de-frise across the river below Philadelphia. Militia drilled in each of the counties. Great consternation was caused in March, 1776, by the appearance of the British vessel, *Roebuck,* in the Bay; several spirited skirmishes shortly took place off New Castle and Lewes. After the Sussex militia had successfully acquitted itself on one such occasion, Dr. James Tilton was lulled into a false security about the patriotism of his neighbors. "Lewistown," he wrote, "is at this time made up of officers and soldiers, and the people altogether seem determined to defend our little place. As for Tories, there are none among us." The militia had promised the British some "Yankee play" if they tried to fish on the beach.[1] Dr. Tilton was mistaken. Even at this early date, deposition of a prisoner held on the *Roebuck* proves that many residents of Sussex County were still faithful to the mother country.[2] A prejudiced Englishman who had escaped from Baltimore jail in January and fled to this loyalist section in order to take a boat back home, saw repeated instances of disaffection. "The principal gentlemen of the county," he recorded in his book published eight years later, "for sixty or eighty miles around came constantly to us in the dead of night in order to assist us and to furnish us with all the intelligence of the country. They acquainted me with the very favourable disposition of a great majority of the inhabitants to his Majesty's government, and requested my directions for their future conduct."[3] When the loyalists began an insurrection at Salisbury, Maryland, in the next county, in February, he advised them to disperse, since they were unsupported and unarmed. If the rebels insisted on bloodshed, however, he intended "to seize on the magazines and artillery in Lewis's Town, to raise and embody all the loyalists in Sussex, and to make use of the most active and vigorous exertions against the common enemy." Fortunately, the Maryland loyalists abandoned their struggle within a short time, and he was not forced to their assistance.[4]   On March 12, he fled from Delaware, accompanied by Thomas Robinson, Boaz Manlove, and a Mr. Kollock.[5]   Probably the British were already recruiting in Sussex County in March, but two months later there is definite knowledge of their success.   Peter Rea, an expelled Maryland loyalist, in search of a friendly refuge like the escaped prisoner from Baltimore jail, received a hearty welcome in lower Delaware.   From the Northeast Fork of the Nanticoke on May 25, he addressed a letter to a British officer, recommending three fine recruits.   They had decided to enlist "to the most Gracious of Sovereign's; rather than to a Number of Tyrants, who exempts themselves from all Restraint of Shame, and overleaps the Bounds of all Law, both humane and divine, and breaks out into the greatest Tyranny and Injustice to every Person they suspect not to have imbibed their most absurd and Rebellious Principals."[6]

The inhabitants of Kent County were scarcely more attached to the Continental Congress.   John Haslet on May 13 was greatly dismayed by a project to exchange Lieutenant Ball captured from the *Roebuck* for an American captain.   Not only had the Lieutenant expressed great satisfaction on finding so many true subjects of his Majesty in the circle of his acquaintances, but knowing their naked and defenseless position, he could find it "in his power with 150 men well armed to desolate [a] great part of this Seemingly Devoted County."[7]   Sir Andrew Snape Hammond, commander of the *Roebuck,* was very anxious to have Ball released.[8]   Even greater disturbance was created by a Congressional resolution in May urging the colonies to form new governments.   "Most of those here whom are *termed the Cool Considerate men,"* Caesar Rodney wrote his brother, "think it amounts to a declaration of Independence.   It Certainly savours of it, but you will see and Judge for Your Self."[9]   Such a radical proposal thoroughly aroused the conservative element, which thus far had attempted no organized resistance.   Thomas Rodney's expectation that the proposal would encounter no opposition in Kent County was unduly optimistic.[10]   The Whigs near Dover prepared to "instruct" their delegation in the Assembly by petition to recommend favorable action or the holding of a constitutional convention. If the legislature refused to listen to reason, the representatives from Kent County were to dissolve the session by withdrawing.[11] When the paper was passed around among Thomas Rodney's militia on May 25, only 28 of the 68 members signed it,[12] though the majority acquiesced in a fortnight.[13] The attitude of the greater part of the inhabitants in lower Delaware was well-known to John Haslet. "A vast majority in Sussex are against . . . " he wrote Caesar Rodney. "[I] fear Congress must either disarm a large Part of Kent & Sussex, or see their Recommendation treated with Contempt."[14] The circulation of counter-resolutions resulted in a riot at Mispillion muster.[15] The Whigs faced an organized opposition for the first time.

The points over which the factions were quarreling are well-revealed in their two documents. The radical petition declared that the present government was "not sufficient to the exigency of our affairs" and urged the Assembly to comply with the suggestion of Congress.[16] The counter-petition stated that the Congressional resolution had been misinterpreted, for it applied only to governments in disorder, "not to those whose Assemblies were competent and adequate." Supposedly, the present unhappy disputes were begun for the defense and preservation of chartered rights, privileges, and existing forms of government; to change the latter during this critical period would disunite the people and be productive of dangerous consequences.[17] Thomas Robinson, who actively circulated the conservative petition in Sussex County, claimed that the Tories secured 5,000 signatures, while the Whigs obtained only 300.[18] Squire John Clark, of Kent County, was chosen to present the document to Congress. On the way he was seized, put in the pillory, and the petition destroyed. His indignant friends rebelled, but the intervention of two ministers saved Dover from the threatening forces.[19] Enoch Anderson, attached to a regiment at Lewes, refers vaguely to this incident in his memoirs.[20] "Thus the first insurrection in *Delaware* happened in the county of Kent."[21]

The Tories in Sussex County instigated a more serious revolt. When Enoch Anderson left Dover for Lewes, he was stopped several times by Tories as one of the "d——d Haslet men"; his company of 300 men was soon surrounded by 1500 Tories who kept in close touch with the British men of war in the Bay.[22]

Some indication that trouble was brewing reached Dover on June 5,[23] but Henry Fisher delayed informing Congress of the difficulty for five days. The presence of numerous Tories on land necessitated sending the message by sea.[24] David Hall, President of the Sussex Council of Safety, also implored aid from Congress lest "their situation would be as calamitous as that of *Norfolk*."[25] The news first reached the Assembly sitting at New Castle on June 13, 1776. Greatly alarmed over the incident, Thomas McKean wrote Congress at 2:30 a. m. that the Kent militia had already been ordered out and that reenforcements from New Castle County would soon follow.[26] At 7:00 p. m. the same day he reported that the insurgents had dispersed after a conference with the local council of safety, though the real cause of the disturbance remained unknown. The Assembly had authorized a committee to quiet the people by persuasion or force.[27] McKean, as well as some of the soldiers from Kent County who had returned before reaching their objective,[28] was misinformed about the withdrawal of the Tories. On June 14, General Rhodes forwarded to Caesar Rodney an urgent message requesting assistance.[29] Congress, wisely enough, had already sent a large force of 3,000 men under Colonel Miles to Lewes; upon its arrival the Tories fled.[30] Scouting expeditions swore the leaders including Robinson to allegiance to Congress before the continental troops departed.[31] When the Constitutional Convention met in August, about fifty residents of Sussex County petitioned for pardon, "now being convinced that it was an open Violation of the Rules and Regulations of the Honourable Continental Congress and the Assembly of this Government, made in Support of American Liberty"; they promised for the future "to support and enforce the Resolutions of these Honourable Bodies." The Assembly granted a full pardon, even restoring arms and reappointing the suspended officers of the militia.[32]

Several causes combine to explain the reasons for the revolt. By June 10, it was a common rumor in Sussex County that "those who oppose all [?] Independence are Libul to be put to Distress"; therefore, William Polk suggsted that the militia officers assemble at Mr. William Bradley's, Sr., to consider the proper way "to oppose these Tiranical Pirates."[33] Apparently, a petition concerning grievances was then addressed to the Council of Safety, for next day David Hall and John Wiltbank replied to William Polk and others: "We know of no intention in the inhabitants of this part of the County of destroying your houses by fire or otherways and are totally strangers with respect to your complaint of a number of guns being taken from you . . . " They promised to make restitution if the claims proved justified.[34] Isaac Bradley in a letter on June 12 considered a local grievance back of the revolt; it was "only to settle Some Internal matters that we think we have been agrieved in and that in order for the settlement of the same we have appointed six men on our Part and the Council of Safety has appointed others on their Part to Settle the Matter."[35] The effort of John Wiltbank, Henry Fisher, and Ward Lewes, at least one of whom was a staunch Whig, "to have the persons lately taken in Custody at Lewis Town upon Suspicion of being Disaffected persons Immediately Discharged and Set at Liberty" also suggests that the quarrel was of domestic origin.[36]

Other contemporaries assign different reasons for the insurrection. Captain Dagworthy in a letter to Colonel Rhodes on June 14 reported the intelligence "that four men had been on board the Ships of War and proposed that in case they would land one hundred men they would be jointed by one thousand for Government and as far as we can learn there Intention is to land near Indian River."[37] On the other hand, a Maryland Tory on board the *Roebuck* put the cart before the horse by recording that the coming of the Continental troops caused the outbreak: "The People about Lewistown having [been] suspected of holding Correspondence with the Men of War in the River by the Congress they sent down 3,000 to disarm and reduce them to obedience. this being known to the people they were ready to arm for the King."[38] "I have the pleasure to inform you," wrote Sir Andrew Snape Hammond on the *Roebuck* to his commander-in-chief on June 24, 1776, "that the inhabitants of the two Lower Counties on the Delaware tired of the Tyranny and oppression of the times have taken up arms to the number of 3 thousand and declared themselves in favour of Government. Three very Sensible Men have been aboard the Liverpool, and declared that with a few Regulars to put them in order they would march directly to Philadelphia with 6 or 7 thousand men that they would raise in a week. The Congress have already taken some Step towards disarming them, but are not in the least likely to succeed." According to Hammond's informants, "a great majority of people on the Eastern Shore of Maryland and in the lower counties of Delaware" were for the British.[39]

Thomas Robinson attributed the outbreak solely to the destruction of the counter-petition. This malicious act resulted in the uprising c. 1500 Tories under his direction "to suppress the Mobs and Lawless Committees and to restore his Majesty's Government within the Delaware Counties."[40] Since this statement proves conclusively that Robinson was present in Delaware in June, his flight in March with several Tory companions must only have been a temporary absence.[41] Several reasons by as many different writers, then, must be combined to explain the Sussex insurrection in June, 1776. Militia grievances, trading with the British men of war, the sending of Continental forces to Lewes, and the destruction of the petition—all contributed something to the spark setting off the rebellion. But the underlying cause was the general opposition to independence.

The mere presence of troops did not quiet the disaffected in Sussex County. On June 20, the very day on which Colonel Miles' battalion arrived at Lewes, David Hall asked the Committee of Public Safety in Philadelphia for several armed barges to protect the sloops in Indian River from enemy vessels, though Captain Lawrence was already doing excellent service in breaking up the illicit trade.[42] On July 5, Hall forwarded to Congress depositions from several Whigs along Broad Creek. On the average in Sussex County they believed "that there is, at least, six disaffected to one man for America." As patriots they applied for protection; else they would be forced "to leave their hivings, or fall and run with the current." "Vast numbers of the inhabitants of Somerset and Dorchester Counties in Maryland, and of Sussex County in Delaware have men on board of these men-of-war and tenders, either trading, enlisting, taking the oath of allegiance, or something we really are not informed of." Tories had uttered many dire threats against the Whigs.[43] A traveler near Cedar Creek in July was informed by four armed men that Lord Dunmore had landed troops in Maryland and that 1500 would assemble in Sussex to aid him.[44] Captain Haslet temporarily sent one company of militia to Broad Creek.[45] But by July 22, the militia companies in all the counties were disbanded, apparently for political reasons due to the approaching election, since the activities of the Tories continued.[46]

THE FORMATION OF THE NEW GOVERNMENT

Meanwhile, the colony continued to drift towards the formation of a new government. The "important business" for which the

Kent County legislators urged the release of Robinson and Moore in March was the consideration of how far the Assembly at that time should proceed with such measures. When the instructions for the delegates in Congress were drawn up, the first clauses directed them to "embrace very favourable opportunity to effect a reconciliation with Great Britain," and sanctioned military operations if necessary. The third clause was an important step towards complete separation from Pennsylvnia; the delegates were told "decently but firmly to urge the Right of this Government to an equal Voice in Congress with any other Province or Government on this Continent."[47] On May 15, Congress recommended the establishment of independent governments. Caesar Rodney thought that the suggestion "savoured" of independence. An endeavor to carry it out was among the sparks setting off the Kent and Sussex rebellions, for both counties opposed the change by large majorities. At the June session of the legislature all mention of reconciliation was omitted in the instructions. In addition to claiming equal voting privileges with other representations, the delegates were told to concur in the ratification of foreign treaties, inter-colonial pacts, and other measures designed to "promote the liberty, safety, and interests of America." In the preamble notice was served that a new government should shortly be set up in accordance with the request of Congress.[48] Before further steps could be taken, the Declaration of Independence had been voted. Contrary to tradition, Caesar Rodney did not arrive in Philadelphia on July 4 just in time to sign the document. It has been conclusively proved that he was present on the second to approve Richard Henry Lee's resolution for independence.[49] The event was celebrated in Dover by "a fine turtle feast."[50] According to legend the committee of public safety also burned a portrait of King George on the Green. The President of this body then said, "Compelled by strong necessity, thus we destroy even the shadow of that King who refused to reign over a free people," and the crowd huzzaed.[51] A meeting of the Assembly in July approved the Declaration of Independence and directed each county to elect ten delegates to a constitutional convention. In order to make certain of their allegiance, voters were required to swear or affirm "to support and maintain the Independence of this Government, as declared by the Honourable Continental Congress."[52] Fortunately, the conservatives preferred to utilize peaceful methods in the political struggle rather than violence.[53]

The campaign can be followed with some detail in Kent County. Both Whigs and Tories made every effort to elect their sympathizers to the convention. The Whigs toyed with the idea of appointing committees to investigate lukewarm individuals, but abandoned the suggestion upon the advice of Caesar Rodney for fear of arousing a vindicative spirit.[54] An address to the inhabitants of Kent County on election morning has been preserved, which seems chiefly notable for its moderate tone,[55] but partisan John Haslet, commenting on the speech and author (Read?), thought that "in one stroke or two, the cunning partisan unmasks himself, in spite of the veil of candour and expansive benevolence, he is at so much paints to put on."[56] The highest Whig candidate polled at least 150 votes less than the lowest Tory victor.[57] New Castle County elected a mixed delegation, including the conservative Read and radical McKean. A double set of returns prevailed in Sussex County, but with the backing of George Read, says Timoleon, the Tories were seated.[58] The Whigs were bitterly disappointd by their complete defeat. Caesar Rodney spoke of the "folly and ingratitude of the people."[59] Probably the violence committed by the militia, the departure of the troops before election day and the general conservative attitude of the inhabitants were the principal reasons for the Whig defeat.

The first task of the convention which met at New Castle on August 27 was the issuing of a Declaration of Rights. This document is of little interest from the point of view of originality since its provisions were largely borrowed from the declarations of other states. It listed many fundamental rights, such as freedom of religion, election, and press, which should not be violated.[60] A bicameral legislature of 21 members in the House and 9 in the Council was set up. A weak governor with the advice and consent of a Privy Council exercised the executive power. Perhaps even worse than the superfluidity of these bodies was the cumbersome judicial system, with its numerous courts and judges. Commendable features were the condemnation of the slave trade and a liberal franchise provision, which excluded few persons on religious grounds. The land and property qualifications for voters under the old government were retained.[61] Probably the severest critic of the new constitution was "Philo-Alethias" in a Pennsylvania newspaper. He especially condemned the multiplicity of legislative bodies. "All these opposite and incoherent powers," he wrote, "in that small and greatly-divided handful must produce endless jars and confusions, till one of these powers becomes an aristocracy, and, like Aaron's serpent, swallows up all the rest or betrays the whole to some foreign power, which we know the present representatives of two of these counties, who have been counted all along enemies to the cause of America, would, if they durst, presently do."[62] John Haslet in New Jersey heard that they had "done as little as possible, & modelled their new government as like the old as maybe."[63] In his opinion, George Read was largely responsible for the disgraceful proceedings; "no Puffing Quack ever exerted more absolute domination over the qualmish stomach of his sick and trembling patient."[64]

Since the constitution retained the old system of government practically unchanged, one might think that the conservatives would accept the document as *fait accompli.* But the Tories in Sussex County continued to express their resentment at the new order. On the day of the election in October for members to the Assembly, Henry Fisher thought that "such a scene of disaffection to the common cause of America, as I think have not been equal'd by any transaction on this Continent since the commencement of the present dispute with Great Britain," took place. Wisely enough the friends of American liberty had decided not to participate in the election, but five or six hundred Tories assembled at Lewes. When Fisher refused the loan of an ax to chop down the Liberty Pole, they threatened to roast him alive on sight. Upon its fall, "the Streets resounded with Huzza for King George and General Howe, execrations against Congress, Whigs, &c," and it was then sold for "Hangman's Wages." At the polling place in the court house one of the mob armed with a big hickory stick allowed only the professed friends of the King to vote. Included in the junto elected were one disarmed during the insurrection and another convicted of being hostile to the Cause before the committee of safety.[65] Fisher was convinced "that if there was only one thousand English troops landed in any place within their reach, they would flock to them almost to a man." Such an event would mean the loss of the county to the Tories, if not of the state, and Pennsylvania would be endangered.[66] Timoleon confirms this account of the election.[67] The commander of the *Roebuck* believed that the people of the lower counties favored the British three to one.[68] Congress sent part of a Virginia regiment to Dover to await developments.[69] Conservatives, such as George Read, immediately complained of the invasion of state rights, since the Assembly had requested no intervention.[70]

The election proceeded no more favorably for the Whigs in the other counties. George Read continued to dominate the delegation from northern Delaware. Shortly before the election in Kent County, the Rev. Samuel Magaw, pastor of the Episcopal Church at Dover, wrote to the Society for the Propagation of the Gospel that his parishioners were largely loyalist. "Through the whole compass of America," he reported, "I do not believe that there can be any where a stronger attachment to the Parent Country, or a more warm regard for that Religion which we jointly profess, than among the greatest number of those to whom I have been appointed Minister. They ardently wish for peace."[71] The election results confirmed his opinion. John Haslet was "much mortified at the amazing revolution of sentiment in the two lower counties. Mobile vulgus. As astonishing is the system of government formed by their representatives so republican . . . What must the constituents think of it, hooping and hollowing for the King?"[72] "How meditated, deep, and pointed, is their malice," he commented to Caesar Rodney a week later, "but for a few friendships, together with the tender charities of the Father and the Husband which draw me by the heart-strings to revisit Kent, I should wish never to see it more."[73] Probably Haslet's feelings were reenforced by the actions of the legislature when it met in November.

THE CONSERVATISM OF THE ASSEMBLY

The election of delegates to the Continental Congress early demonstrated its conservative leanings. The radical Caesar Rodney and McKean were replaced by the conservative Evans and Dickinson, while Read was continued in office. The lukewarm John McKinly was elected President of the new government in February. This was an unfortunate choice, since he did not whole-heartedly approve of the measures advocated by Congress. Even before his election he was accused of dissuading the New Castle militia from marching upon an important occasion.[74] In spite of continued evidence of disaffection in Sussex County in May, 1777, he believed the reports "without foundation" and received a well-merited rebuke from Congress.[75] During his imprisonment by the British he was reported lodging "at widow Jenkin's, along with his *old friends* Robinson and Manlove, and seemed *very happy.*"[76]   How the extreme Whigs regarded his choice is revealed in a letter written by John Haslet, who got wind of his nomination in November.   "I am informed," he wrote Caesar Rodney, "that the Arch-Politican [Read] has refused the Government, and intends it I'm told for the blundering Br———er [McKinly]. he will then govern the old Woman and State; and, retired, behind the scene, will be blamed for nothing.[77]   When Thomas Rodney heard of the appointment by a vote of 19 to 4, he wrote his brother, "I think they have been very exact in their Choice as he is the only man that could so fully represent The Whig and Tory Complexion of this State—I make no doubt all their appointments will be of a peice with this and that the State will Continue in the same shackling condition it has been in some time past—without affoarding the least aid to the Union except the private influence of a few individuals———."[78]

Perhaps the worst appointments by the new Assembly were the judges.   Timoleon has left a picturesque description of their character, which is confirmed in general by other accounts.   Only in New Castle County were Whig appointments made; in lower Delaware out-and-out Tories were selected.

> In Kent county, the chief justice appointed to the pleas was a man too honest, and consequently possessed of too squeamish a conscience, to swear to maintain a government which he wished never to be established: he therefore declined to take the oaths.   The famous Clark, who had been pilloried and egged at Dover, was appointed second justice.   A noted bully, who, on all occasions, cursed the Bostonians as rebels and traitors, and had fortified his house with loop-holes and guns, for his defence against whigs and committees, was appointed third justice.   And a man, detained for a long time under guard, by General Smallwood, for a well grounded suspicion of traiterous and treasonable practices, was appointed fourth justice.   Some time afterwards, Clark was advanced to the place of chief justice, and his place of second justice, was filled by a man, who, at the same time Clark was pilloried, escaped from a window, from fear, excited by conscious guilt only, and hiding in the swamps, did not dare to come forth, until he had written the most abject concessions to the captain of the light infantry.[79]

Of the original choices it is known from other sources that the chief justice fled to the British lines,[80] that the second justice had participated in the Kent insurrection of 1776 and was paroled for Tory activity in 1781,[81] that the third had exhibited conservative, if not loyalist, tendencies,[82] and that the fourth was confined for some time in 1778 on suspicion.[83] The record speaks for itself.

Equally bad were the selections in Tory-ridden Sussex County. The chief justice was a former captain of the militia, who had vainly tried to persuade his soldiers to engage in an insurrection, had plundered his neighbors of arms, and was placed on the black list of 1776.[84] His colleagues exhibited like talents; two had participated in the first Sussex rebellion.[85] Continental officers who captured loyalists in this section found it necessary to send their prisoners directly to Congress, since there was "no great probability that Tory judges will punish Tory offenders."[86] Chief Justice Killen of the Supreme Court confessed to sympathetic George Read in August, 1777, that he regarded his task as "really too arduous," for in attempting to execute it, he experienced "both a want of knowledge and firmness of mind."[87] The Whig assembly in the next session wrote its own indictment of the judicial appointments.[88] Thomas McKean, speaker of the house at this time, believed only six members could be classified as patriots;[89] to the people's choice of representatives and the Assembly's selection of officials he laid the blame for Delaware's misfortunes in the next few years.[90] Thomas Rodney noted in May, 1777, that "from the choice of the Convention to your present sessions we had not a whig in the General Assembly from this county or Sussex" and that the residents in those counties selected for office those notoriously distinguished for their Torism."[91]

The action of the legislature in a number of minor matters demonstrates its conservative tendencies. Discarding good evidence, it disproved charges of selling poultry to the *Roebuck* and *Pearl* lodged against Daniel Dingee, a member of the legislative council from Sussex County.[92] When the cry of state rights freed four Delaware Tories held in the Pennsylvania jail, no steps were taken to punish them.[93] After both had fled from Sussex County, the arrests of Boaz Manlove, county treasurer, for the embezzlement of £387 and of Thomas Robinson as an enemy of the American Cause were ordered.[94] Apparently, no action was taken in the case of Joseph Cord of Sussex County, who aided two prisoners from the Baltimore jail in escaping to the *Roebuck*.[95] Without any attempts at chastisement, the lenient members courteously returned two letters confiscated from the Rev. Samuel Tingley, Episcopalian rector at Lewes.[96] By these acts the legislature appears condemned for inefficiency and Toryism.

Perhaps public pressure forced this body to pass the first general measure against the loyalists. It was entitled "An Act to Punish Treason and Disaffected Persons, and for the Security of the Government." The preamble read, "Whereas, in the present Time of Danger the Safety of the People more especially requires, That all Persons who are so wicked as to devise the Destruction of Good Government, or to aid or assist the Enemies of the State, shall suffer condine Punishment." By the affirmations or oaths of two witnesses, persons might be convicted of carrying on war against the state or adhering to the King; such traitors should suffer death without benefit of clergy and the forfeiture of their lands and chattels except for the dowry of the widow. Anyone who preached, wrote, or affirmed King or Parliament should be fined.[97] This last provision effectively silenced Episcopalian ministers. But the Tories remained active.

The Continental Congress in April feared disturbances in Sussex County and the adjacent parts of Maryland. Acting upon information furnished by the Maryland delegates, it urged the Assembly to imprison all insurgents, confiscate their property, and appoint commissioners to detect dastardly plots; 100 soldiers to co-operate with the Maryland and Continental troops in the area were requested.[98] When McKinly submitted the recommendation to the House on May 10, he reported that an investigation disclosed that the inhabitants were "very quiet" and the suspicion unfounded.[99] Nevertheless, the House directed McKinly with the concurrence of the Privy Council to send a committee of three to Sussex County.[100] Its findings revealed "that a considerable part of the Inhabitants of that County are unfriendly & disaffected to the present Constitution of the Government in this State, and to the Independence of the United States in general." An active trade and correspondence with the British men-of-war were kept up.[101] The Assembly adjourned without having taken cognizance of tht report.

CONTINUED DISAFFECTION

Patriotic citizens of Sussex County were disgusted at the evasive stand of the legislature. On June 24, David Hall and some other residents complained to the President of Congress that the Assembly had taken no steps to quiet the loyalists, while the treason law was disregarded by filling the civil offices with persons "notorious for their opposition to the Independence of this State," and the disaffected continued their traffic with the British in provisions. So bold had the Tories and British become "in this iniquitous Trade, that they fish and fowl together in common along the Shore." Sixty men from the upper part of the county had recently been recruited by the enemy. A new scheme "deterious" to American liberty was being tried, for Simon Kollock, assisted by the sheriff, Dorman Lofland, was purchasing cattle for the hated Englishmen with £70,000 of counterfeit American money. The signers had "not the least reason to doubt, that if the Enemy were to gain the smallest advantage over the Army of the United American States, and the English appear on our Coast, that there would be a general rising in favour of the British King and his forces."[102] After receipt of this letter Congress condemned the Assembly for its ineffective treason law and its failure to act upon a report from some of its own members.[103] Finally, Maryland troops under Colonel Richardson as well as 200 of the Delaware militia were sent "Tory-catching" in Sussex County.[104]

Caesar Rodney as Brigadier-General for Kent and part of Sussex had been ferreting out Tories for several months. Centers for their activities were along the Mispillion, Duck and Murderkill Creeks. McKinly particularly desired the capture of one "red full-faced old fellow of the two-masted Boat from Murder Kill & his tall son with the rough, scurfy, sun-tanned face," both of whom had been a good deal of a nuisance.[105] General Rodney in July captured Jonas Edinfield and John Ashworthy of Bombay Hook and John Conner of Thoroughfare Neck, who had been trading in cattle. Conner had also piloted the enemy's barges up Duck Creek on a privateering expedition.[106] Chief Justice Killen was not anxious to press the charges against loyalists like Edingfield, who (as an excuse) had to support a wife, an aged mother, and seven children. "Also what offence is he guilty of who is apprehended with live stock and sundry other provisions on his way to traffic with the enemies of the State, and acknowledges that that was his intention?" he asked George Read. He confessed to "both a want of knowledge and firmness of mind—the latter most"—in executing his new office.[107] In Mispillion Neck trading had become such an evil that patriots feared to inform on Tory neighbors.[108]

As usual, Sussex County in which both Rodney and Richardson were active was the worst offender. On one occasion, the Tories even topped Rodney's reward for information.[109] At the end of July, Rodney seized 20 or 30 loyalists, who were trading with the enemy in the upper part of the county. With their two cartloads of sheep, poultry, and fruit, they were taken to Dover jail.[110] On the next evening he had intended to use their signals to decoy the enemy ashore, but on the way he was told that a number of outraged Sussex Countians had assembled to march against Dover. About ten of the thirty persons gathered for this person were imprisoned.[111] Chief Justice Killen lived in continual fear that on some unlucky night the bullying, swearing fellows from the British ships might invade Dover, "for ever since the apprehending [of] the criminals in our jail . . . we have been threatened by the men-of-wars' people with the most direful vengeance, through resentment for confining their friends in prison."[112] Other cases concerning Tories came before the Chief Justice during the summer, but the violators of the treason law escaped after posting recognizances.[113] Catching Tories, as Killen observed, was like cutting off the hydra's head.[114]

Colonel Richardson also found his hands full in Sussex County. Basing his opinion on the best information and his own observations, he reported to Congress that " a large Majority of the Inhabitants of the County are disaffected; and would I believe afford the Enemy every Aid in their Power, except Personal Service in the Field, which the greater part of them want Spirit to do." Captain Murphy had recently captured a sloop from New York and obtained several letters addressed to Sussex residents, including Peter and Burton Robinson. Since there was "no great probability that Tory Judges will punish Tory offenders however Atrocious their offence," he had sent these two persons under guard to Congress. Richardson had also apprehended Thomas Lightfoot and Thomas Cockayne, who had in their possession 199 thirty-dollar counterfeit bills, obtained from Simon Kollock; he was close on the trail of that "Atrocious Villain," Sheriff Dorman Lofland, who had been chased into a large swamp. So far he had received no aid from the Delaware militia, but he hoped for the support of ten or twenty light horse.[115] The loyalists in Sussex County were bitterly disappointed in August when the British fleet failed to sail up the Delaware River. Several pilots from Lewes joined it.[116] Thomas Robinson on board one of the ships regretted that Howe vetoed his plan to land with 500 soldiers and recruit an army of 6,000 which would meet Howe in New Castle County after marching through the lower part of the state.[117] Howe had seriously considered landing at New Castle or Wilmington, and Sir Andrew

Snape Hammond, commander of the *Roebuck,* had urged that the troops be disembarked at New Castle with the transports left behind at Reedy Island, but Howe, because of expected opposition from American forces at either of those two towns, selected the shallower Chesapeake.[118]

CHAPTER III.

The Critical Period

THE BRITISH INVASION

*T*HE landing of the British at the Head of the Elk late in August shifted the attention of the state government for the moment from catching Tories in Kent and Sussex Counties to cooperation for defense with the Continental troops. As Howe advanced, Washington steadily retreated until he reached the banks of the Brandywine on September 11. For the most part, the inhabitants of the invaded district remained quietly at home, following a policy of peaceful non-intervention. A spirited skirmish took place at Cooch's Bridge, in which forty Americans were killed or wounded. Many more on both sides were killed or wounded at the battle of Brandywine in which Washington was defeated and forced to withdraw toward Philadelphia. Wilmington was temporarily occupied by Howe's soldiers, and President McKinly captured. Great damage to buildings and crops was committed by both armies; the historian especially regrets the seizure by the British of Delaware colonial and state archives. Emboldened by the presence of their allies, a great group of unsuspected Tories appeared, and many followed the British army to Philadelphia. John Watson, "physicist" of New Castle, for example, was mobbed and insulted until he welcomed the chance to join Howe. During the British occupation he temporarily promoted an association of loyalists, and later in the spring of 1778, Thomas Slater of Newport and he fitted out a galley to capture "some of the most troublesome and inveterate Rebels of their Acquaintance."[1] John Drake, an innkeeper of New Castle, had sold his belongings in April, 1776, and "skulked" at the home of friends until the English army passed by.[2] Benjamin Galloway, a fisherman from Kent County, imprisoned because he refused to drill with the militia, joined the enemy at Wilmington and raised

27

recruits for Colonel Chamber's regiment.[3] Within a few weeks
the British army, slightly swelled by additions from the Delaware
loyalists, left New Castle County in their only campaign on
Delaware soil during the Revolution. An uprising in lower
Delaware had been expected, but none occurred. Apparently,
General Rodney was misinformd in writing Washington that some
Methodists in western Kent County were encouraging the inhabitants to revolt.[4] Thus passed the most favorable opportunity for
a successful insurrection.[5]

AFTERMATH

The critical period during the War for Delaware was the following winter. Thomas McKean, temporarily summoned to lead the
government, deplored the general lack of enthusiasm for independence. For the moment he was delaying to assume the easy
office of Chief Justice of Pennsylvania, in order "to step forth to
save 'a poor distressed State' without a head, without a shilling,
public records in possession of the enemy, together with their
capital & principal trading town; the militia dispirited and dispersed, many of them fled out of the State for safety, and a majority
of the rest supposed to be disaffected to the glorious cause we are
engaged in."[6] The New Castle County courts were jammed with
a multitude of cases concerning Tories in November. Charles
Bryson was indicted for saying "that he dealt with the enemy &
would do it again and that he had taken Protection under the
Crown & would Defend it."[7] Jesper Beeson revealed that many
of his friends as well as himself had sold cattle to the British;[8]
as late as 1783 he was still petitioning for payment.[9] Jacob
Derrickson, John and William Almond, and Joseph Judson, all of
whom participated in the illicit trade, were named in the excepted
list of the treason act of 1778.[10] George Read in December was
alarmed by "the frequent landing of the enemy of late in the neighborhood of Port Penn, and the little opposition they met with";
he feared an attack from that quarter.[11] The British invasion
had revealed an astounding number of loyalists in New Castle
County. A British officer stationed off the town of New Castle in
October, 1777, observed that the people in the three lower counties
"are certainly well-affected in general, and have brought us large
supplies of everything we wanted."[12]

Few cases of prosecution in these arduous times are on record
in the lower counties. The six principals engaged in the trade

with the enemy along Duck Creek were sent to Brigadier-General Patterson, while a larger number were freed.[13] Since the activities of the Tories in that vicinity still continued, Caesar Rodney found it necessary to employ 100 men "in keeping in awe and preventing the disaffected carrying on Trade with and Supplying the Enemy with Provisions."[14] Several other persons in Kent County were convicted of levying war against the State or selling corn to the to the British.[15] No record of Tory offenses in Sussex County exists, but the election in October gave ample opportunity for the inhabitants to reveal their feelings. Congress in November requested McKean "to exert his utmost Endeavors effectually to prevent the disaffected Inhabitants of that State from furnishing the Enemies Fleet or Army wih Provisions or Supplies of any Kind."[16] A month later, the fear that the British might establish a post at Wilmington to draw food-stuffs from Delaware and countenance the disaffected caused Congress to station General Smallwood there as a preventive measure.[17]

A revulsion of feeling in October after the Battle of Brandywine resulted in strong Whig delegations from New Castle and Kent Counties, but a riot in Sussex County prevented any election. Previously, wild rumors had circulated in this district that, if the Whigs, won the militia would be drafted and compelled to go to camp. On election day the Tories came to Lewes by the hundreds and then began "in their usual strain of drinking prosperity to King George, Damning the Whigs, and swearing there was not Rebels enough in Town to take them up, &c." When the Whigs tried to enforce the taking of a patriotic oath, the enraged Tories threatened to throw them "Neck and Heels out of the Court-House." The election inspectors present might have accepted the suggestion, but Jacobs Moore and John Wiltband intervened. Moore had opposed such an oath in the Assembly and with 150 others threatened to sue if such action were taken. The Whigs then addressed a note to the sheriff, insisting that the oath be administered. In a letter composed by Moore, the sheriff replied that the use of force would compel the adjournment of the election. After Major Henry Fisher delivered the next Whig epistle, which demanded the taking of the oath or adjournment, "else I will make Lewes Town too Hot for every Tory in it," Isaac Bradley and others assaulted him with fists, clubs, and feet. Scarcely had the militia rescued him, or "he must have been murdered in a few minutes more," when the Whigs attacked the Tories. A gun was fired at Bradley, and the Tories fled through the windows of the courthouse pursued by the militia.[18] The rump legislature dealt only with urgent business until a delegation appeared from Sussex County.

The Whigs were thoroughly discouraged in the winter of 1778 by the British invasion and the prevalent disaffection. General-Brigadier Patterson wrote to Thomas McKean in January, "in fact we are all going to the vengeance. I cannot see what will save us. Tories taken up every day. discharg'd on recognizance and trade again. No jail to secure any person. No records and no withall [?], or officers to execute anything."[19] Though McKean no longer headed the govrenment, he was still concerned about the welfare of the State. "The situation of Delaware gives me constant anxiety," he wrote Read in February. "The choice of representatives in October, 1776, and their choice of officers, have occasioned all its misfortunes. Nothing but effectual laws vigorously executed, can possibly save it, and there seems to me not the least prospect of the former, and when I learn that not a single step is taken towards collecting the fines under the present inadequate militia law, or to punish the most impudent traitors, or even the harboring of deserters, I despair of any law, tending to support the freedom, independence, and sovereignity of the State, being executed, especially in Kent and Sussex." The captured president was reported to be lodging in Philadelphia with his old Tory friends, Robinson and Manlove, and seemed *"very happy."*[20]

Yet in these darkest moments, some of the Whigs did not despair. Oddly enough, Brigadier-General Patterson, who had addressed such a pessimistic note to McKean in January, wrote in a different vein to General Rodney in the same month: "Never was America in so fair a way to compleat the grand Struggle in our favour from every quarter and Accompts."[21] The election of staunch Whigs—Rodney, McKean, and VanDyke—to the Continental Congress in December, in place of Read, Evans, and Dickinson cheered many. Those who believed in prophecies might have been comforted by the death-bed vision of Elizabeth Shipley, Quaker leader, for she foretold "that the invader of our land shall be driven back." After the story had been published in a New Jersey newspaper, the Tory *Pennsylvania Ledger* commented on the anxiety of the Whigs to believe any idle tales that might further their cause.[22] Undoubtedly, the most encouraging news was the election of a Whig delegation from Sussex County in March by what the Whigs regarded as a miracle. Perhaps the law passed in the previous session, which required all voters to take an oath of allegiance, had something to do with the returns. Timoleon wrote, "So many of the disaffected in Sussex had refused to take the test necessary to qualify them to vote, that the whigs of that county had uniformly carried their ticket from the year 1777 until October 1785."[23] In great jubilation, General Rodney informed McKean of the happy event: "These men joined with the representation from Newcastle county, you'l be apt to think with me, will produce not only wholesome Laws & Regulations but Energy in the Execution of them, and thereby rouse this little Branch of the Union from its heretofore Torpid State, which God of his Infinite Mercy Grant—I need not tell you How disagreeable the Scituation of those in this Peninsula, who Openly profess friendship to the American Cause, a narrow neck of Land liable to the incursions of the Enemy, by water in small Parties, and therefore their property Exposed."[24]

THE WHIG ASSEMBLY OF 1778

With the aid of the Whigs from Sussex, the assembly proceeded to enact vigorous laws against the Tories. Being "fully convinced that some of the disaffected inhabitants of Sussex have taken up arms, much to the terror of the good people of said county and the encouragement of the British forces to land and make excursions," it ordered General Dagworthy to move against the Tories.[25] Supposedly on the grounds that they lived in the same county, the resignations of Supreme Court Justices Killen and Cooke were requested, but the significantly-worded preamble was a sad commentary on the judges appointed in the preceding year:

> The late appointment of Judges and Justices for some of the said Courts hath not produced the said salutary effects, inasmuch as the place of residence of some is by no means calculated for the most easy and convenient administration of justice; others of them, so appointed, have neglected to accept of the places to which they were appointed, and, being unfriendly to the freedom and independence of the United States, and the Government of this State in particular, have fled to the open enemies thereof; and many of them that did accept have neglected to enforce the laws of the State, to punish treason and traitorous practices, to preserve the peace, to punish harbourers of deserters.[26]

Brigadier-General Patterson objected to the seating of a member from Kent County because Captain Allen McLane had inserted an advertisement in the *Pennsylvania Packet* for the apprehension of a deserter, last "seen at Little-Creek Neck in the said County in Company with Jacob Stout Esq., a member of the Assembly and Justice of Peace for said County."[27] Stout absented himself from the legislature henceforth. In March Caesar Rodney became president of the State by a vote of 20 to 4. Under his vigorous administration, the disaffected were at last cowed.

The most important work of the session was the passage of three laws dealing with the Tories. An act for the further security of the government required every male white over 21 to appear before a Justice of Peace by July 1 and take an oath of allegiance to the government. Those refusing were forbidden to hold any civil or military office, exercise the suffrage, or serve as jurymen.[28] A second act confiscated the supplies, horses, and boats of loyalists caught trading with the British.[29] The most important measure was entitled "An Act of Free Pardon and Oblivion." With the exception of 46 loyalists, offenders against freedom were restored to their estates and pardoned if by August 1 they should appear before a Justice of the Supreme Court or of the Peace and take an oath of allegiance. They would remain forever incapable of holding civil or military office and of exercising the suffrage. Offenders who refused to take the oath by that date would lose all real and personal property, which would be sold by commissioners. The wife and children of such persons would receive maintenance money from the sale of the property. Among the prominent loyalists excepted from pardon in New Castle County were Joshua North, William and John Almond, John Drake, John Watson, and Charles Gordon; in Kent, Cheney Clow, William Burrows, Simon VanWinkle, and Prestly Allee; in Sussex, Thomas Robinson, Joshua Hill, James Rench, Boaz Manlove, Dorman Lofland, Abraham Wiltbank, and Simon Kollock.[30] This piece of legislation was deemed effective enough to deal with the loyalists during the remainder of the War.

The provisions of these laws concerning taking the oath of allegiance, furnishing dependents with maintenance money, and confiscating property were not well enforced; moreover, the courts had not been directed about what to do with those excepted from pardon. In 1779, for example, some citizens of Kent County complained that 116 voters in the October election had not been administered the oath.[31]   The commissioners appointed to distribute part of the funds from the sale of property to wives and children seem to have required that the acceptors disown the loyalist husband or father.   Apparently, for this reason dependents of such loyalists as Christopher Wilson, Charles Gordon, Jacob Derrickson, John Gregory, and Joshua North up to January, 1781, had refused all payments.   Mrs. North petitioned the Assembly several times for a settlement of her claim, but the body said that it had offered her £3,000 in 1780, which she had refused.[32]   Delaware was noted for its mild enforcement of its confiscation act.   After the British evacuation of New York in 1783, the Rev. Mr. Addison of Prince George's County, Maryland, returned to Sussex County "thinking it barely not impossible to recover some of the Wreck of his Fortune which had escaped Confiscation in the State of Delaware."[33] Dr. James Rench, of Sussex County, had his possessions restored in 1787.[34]   Even the descendants of Boaz Manlove and Cheney Clow asked for reimbursement.[35]   Perhaps as many as fifty loyalists had property confiscated, but in proportion to their number in the population, the amount seized from them was small.   By October, 1778, the commissioner for New Castle County had obtained £8,060 from his sales;[36] in January, 1781, his total was £52,642.[37]   The wealthiest loyalist in New Castle County appears to have been Joshua North.   No figures for Kent County exist, but because of its general poverty and small population, one can estimate with some degree of accuracy that the revenue from this source was less than in the other counties.   By December, 1781, the commissioner in Sussex County had made returns of £43,300.[38] Thomas Robinson's property brought £34,177; Joshua Hill's, £5,194; Boaz Manlove's, £2,000.   The remainder of the sales is for considerably smaller amounts.[39]

The courts were sorely puzzled by the cases of the loyalists excepted from pardon that came before them.   The records of the Court of Oyer and Terminer for Kent County indicate that the customary procedure was to try the excepted loyalists for treason. Following this procedure, the court found Simon VanWinkle, James Barcus, William Burrows, and Presley Allee not guilty in July, 1778; they were freed on payment of the costs of prosecution.[40]   In spite of defects, the loyalist acts of 1778 worked fairly well in achieving their object of lessening Tory activities.   In addition, perhaps £150,000 in revenue was obtained from the sale of their property.   The Assembly, among whose members were many conservatives throughout the War, did not wish to press very severely against moderate Tories. Upon the passage of the confiscation act in June, 1778, Theodore Maurice, holder of many Crown offices in New Castle County, had fled behind the British lines, seeing the hopelessness of restoring His Majesty's government. Testifying concerning his claim for redress, Joseph Galloway believed that "he might remain there quietly without trimming— as they were moderate People in the Delaware Government— There was throughout the War a Majority of the Assembly in favor of retaining their Allegiance, but it was a small Gov't surrounded by larger ones and incapable of acting of itself."[41] Other factors as well as the treason laws contributed to the decrease in the number of Tory outbreaks. The British had repeatedly failed to aid them in insurrection and had passed them by on their march to Philadelphia; many of their leaders had fled; since they could not take the oath of allegiance, they were excluded from exercising the franchise; the militia and continental forces continually harassed them; in brief, their morale was broken. The passage of the loyalist acts and other events combined to lessen Tory activities subsequent to 1778.

CHENEY CLOW'S REBELLION

The first person named in the excepted list from Kent County was the notorious Cheney Clow, who had instigated a revolt in April, 1778, during the meeting of the legislature. An earlier writer on the incident has proclaimed, "Cheney Clow's rebellion is a Delaware myth. Cheney Clow's fort is equally mythical."[42] Both of these statements are completely erroneous; the writer has confused Clow's actual capture in 1782 with his earlier rebellion, and the site of his fort may still be seen near Kenton. The recent publication of documents has solved the mystery. A picturesque letter written by Colonel Pope describes the initial encounter in the middle of April. When Pope approached the fortification with a small force, 100 insurgents sallied forth to exchange pistol shots. He hastily retreated and assembled a larger expedition.[43] Meanwhile, the frightened Tories fled. On its second trip the militia burned the "fort" and recovered some stolen goods.[44] If "the back-sliding Methodist" had been allowed to continue his efforts, it was expected that he would march against Dover, where the legislature was sitting.[45] About fifty of the participants were later apprehended, and twenty sent off to enlist![46] Clow was not captured until 1782, when a sheriff's posse surrounded his home; in the scuffle one man named Joseph Moore was killed. Claiming that he was a British officer, Clow was freed of the charge of treason, but held on the impossibly high bail of £10,000[47] until indicted on flimsy evidence of murder. There is some reason to believe that Moore was shot by one of the sheriff's own men. Supposedly, Thomas Rodney expressed sympathy for Clow, saying that he was unjustly accused and should be released. Governor Collins stayed his execution, but his successor in 1788 finally sacrificed this scapegoat to public opinion. By 1790 his his heir was petitioning for a restoration of his property.[48] Thus ended Clow's rebellion, around which Delawareans have cast a cloak of romanticism.[49]

DISAFFECTION IN OTHER SECTIONS

This incident was only the most outstanding of numerous Tory outbreaks in 1778. A detachment from General Smallwood's post at Wilmington captured about 40 British sailors and officers in lower New Castle County in March.[50] Delegates in Congress were alarmed by an insurrection at Jordan's Island in April;[51] a punitive expedition seized two British naval officers, eleven marines, and seventy Tories on this occasion.[52] Kent County remained infested with the disaffected. President Rodney regretfully noted at Dover, "We are Constantly Alarmed in this Place by the Enemy and Refugees. and Seldom a day passes but Some man in this and the Neighboring Counties is taken off by these Villians. so that men, near the Bay, Who I know to be hearty in the Cause, dare neither Act or Speak least they Should be taken away and their Houses plundered." He begged McKean to ask Congress for a battalion to aid in the suppression of the Tories, such as the one posted in Sussex County. The practice of taking men from their beds had gone far enough.[53] At the request of the sorely harassed residents of Murderkill and Jones' Necks, the Legislative Council stationed militia in those areas.[54] Writing to the Society for the Propagation of the Gospel in October, 1778, the Rev. Sydenham Thorne of St. Paul's Church in lower Kent County was able to report: "He has been very happy in residing among a people distinguished for their Loyalty & Affection to the British Constitution; and he cannot recollect a single member belonging to either of his congregations who hath taken an active part against the

Government."[55]   Very slowly did the Tories lose their ardor for the British cause.

Sussex County remained the center of the disaffection.   That the enemy was still recruiting with success within its boundaries was the belief of Maryland officials in February.[56]   As the drive of the militia and committees of public safety continued against the loyalists, many, though less obnoxious than Thomas Robinson, fled to New York.   Joshua Hill passed through a grueling experience before he reached the welcome haven of the *Roebuck*.   Several times he was brought before committees for refusing to take the oath of allegiance.   Finally, on March 15, 1778, a party of rebels surrounded his home, and he concealed himself in the woods for four months.   After much discomfort he boarded the *Roebuck*.[57] When an English ship was shipwrecked on the coast of New Jersey in October, the captured pilot revealed a plan to land 700 refugees near Cape Henlopen, "where they expect to be joined by a very considerable part of the inhabitants."[58]   The scheme failed to mature.

The few Whigs in Sussex County were greatly alarmed by the continued disaffection.   The Rev. Matthew Wilson of the Presbyterian Church at Lewes suggested an ingenious way to end the danger in a letter to the Board of War in July, 1778:[59]

> We are informed that some few of our *Sussex Tories* have fallen into your hands, and are justly confined in Jail, where they are much more likely to have an Impartial Trial than here, where at least two-thirds of the County, by the Influence, Lies, Falsewoods, & base insinuations of your Joshua Fisher and about a score of leading Men, who at that Time, held all Offices and Places of Trust in this County, are really disaffected to the American Cause, Yet, by their numbers will soon be elected to fill their places again; so that if this State can do any harm to the Cause of America, by betraying the French, our Friends, or any of the Whig Colonies trading here, or by assisting, supporting, or encouraging our enemies, as well as persecuting for ever the Whigs here, "who have borne the burden and heat of the day," there are more horrors than I can now forsee, must come from the Tories ruling the Delaware State.
>
> I can see only two plans that appear practicable, either to disfranchise the Delaware State, and divide it between Maryland and Pennsylvania, which appears more necessary, because the State is too weak to bear the expense of its present Government, and also because of its smallness: any contention here between a leading Whig and leading Tory would im-

mediately divide the whole State into two parties, when Justice and Peace would be excluded from the State.

The other remedy would only be partial and temporary, i.e., The Congress fixing such Resolves, by such accurate Descriptions of Characters as would exclude all Tories and disaffected persons from holding any office in the State during this Generation at least.

Even if this last plan were adopted, Wilson continued, he still feared that the most artful and dangerous Tories would remain at large; they would continue to use the lesser fry as "Cat's-paws," and no evidence would be secured against them. Therefore, he urged the release of James Couper, held in a Philadelphia jail, for he might be persuaded to give evidence against others. Neither of his ingenious proposals was acted upon.

CHAPTER IV.

The End of the Revolution

THE DECREASE OF TORY ACTIVITY AFTER 1778

DURING the remainder of the Revolution, with the exception of the Sussex insurrection of 1780, the record of loyalist activities in Delaware is singularly unexciting. No longer are the correspondence of Caesar Rodney, the proceedings of the legislature, and the pages of the Delaware Archives filled with accounts of Tories. In contrast to former years, virtually no disturbances occurred in 1779. As it has been pointed out, the passage of the treason acts combined with other factors, such as disfranchisement, lack of British support, and the flight of leaders, to end the Tory menace. The disaffected who continued to reside in Delaware engaged in subterranean plotting, of which little has come to light. A renewed nuisance on an enlarged scale was the audacious attacks of privateering vessels manned by refugees; isolated farmhouses along creeks or near the Bay invited plundering. With the capture of Burgoyne's forces, the alliance with France, and indications that the English would not speedily conquer their rebelling dependency, the Tories subsided into a watchful silence, still confident that victory hovered around the corner—but it never came.

THE BLACK CAMP REBELLION

In August, 1780, the last serious disturbance by the Tories took place. John Jones informed President Rodney that several hundred of the disaffected had been roaming around Sussex County, disarming Whigs, seizing ammunition, and threatening worse things. Before an energetic pursuit from swamp to swamp had dispersed them, five different parties sent out to gain intelligence had been captured.[1] At Rodney's suggestion John Collins investigated; he discovered that the insurgents had first associated in June to oppose the civil law and later had begun to drill under Battholomew Banum. In the early part of August, about 100 had assembled, in order to rob the inhabitants of arms and to kidnap the militia officers. A rumor circulated that the southern part of the peninsula had already rebelled. Perhaps 400 participated in the insurrection, and most of these gathered at Black Camp.[2] Some desired the King's law; some intended to defy all law; others opposed the payment of taxes. Numerous residents explained their reasons for joining the revolt. Levey Messick was told "that the Black camp men was rising to beat down the Tax laws and make the Rich pay as much on the pound rate as the poor & [he] must go with them or they all be killed up totally for the whigs was there upon the Black Camp People daly."[3] Under such pressure he naturally went to the Tory rendezvous. John Riley joined after hearing a report of the true conditions in his county; "the Common Conversation was the Whigs was Mobing the Torys, and catching and swaring of them, to be true to the State and finally taking all the Torys Livings."[4] For participating in the rebellion, thirty-seven persons were indicted before the Justices of the Supreme Court in October, 1780.[5] The legislature offered a reward of $50 for the apprehension of the ring-leader, Battholomew Banum.[6] A ghastly fate was decreed for the principals; eight were ordered to be hung "by the Neck but not till you be dead, for then your Bowels must be taken out, and burnt before your face, then your head must be severed from your body, & your body divided into four Quarters, and these must be at the disposal of the Supreme Authority of the State."[7] Apparently, all the participants were later pardoned by the lenient legislature.[8] Resentment against high taxes and the snooping activities of the militia seem to have been the main causes of the insurrection.

REFUGEE ATTACKS

A series of scattered incidents complete the account of Tory disturbances. Small bands of refugees who frequented the Bay, ready to swoop down on the inhabitants in surprise attacks, were the worst pest. In August, 1780, such a group seized a shallop loaded with wheat in Duck Creek and damaged several other vessels; prompt pursuit by Colonel Pope forced them to beach their prize and flee to the swamps.[9] One audacious band dared to land in Dover Hundred in the daytime, march three miles through the woods, and plunder the country-seat of John Dickinson of plate, wearing apparel, and provisions to the value of £2,000.[10] A slight insurrection occurred in Sussex County in September, 1781, but nothing of its nature is known.[11] At the beginning of 1782, a schooner named *Kitty Meade* was captured near Little Creek, and several persons wounded.[12]

Occasionally, instances of great cruelty occurred, when the refugees bore personal grudges against their prisoners. Because Robert Appleton, a constable of lower New Castle, performed his duties with much officiousness, a band of refugees plundered his home, maltreated his brother, and carried the constable himself away as a captive. Upon reaching Bombay Hook, they "were joined by one Captain Brooks, and five more pirates, who have infested our shores for some time past, which proved an unfortunate junction for the prisoner. He was carried to the house of R. Pearson, placed on a table, and ordered to preach a methodist sermon, they having discovered by papers found on him that he was of that society. On his refusing to preach, Brooks ordered him to be whipt to death, for a damned rebel; a rope of better than an inch thick, which they called a colt, was prepared and a negro brought forward to execute this cruel order." Alternately the refugees beat him until he was exhausted; then he was forced to destroy his official papers and promise that he would never serve the rebels again. He was finally released at Thorough-Fare Point on Duck Creek, where the refugees burned the houses at the landing and destroyed 20 cords of wood.[13] When the same unpopular Appleton tried to serve a warrant on Mr. Codrick, of Bombay Hook, a few weeks later, he received another beating.[14] As late as January, 1783, the refugees continued troublesome; at that time the Duke de Luzan was summoned to dislodge a group near Duck Creek.[15] Undoubtedly, the blame for all these outrages cannot be laid to the Delaware loyalists or refugees, for some were obviously committed by "pirates," but in others their hand is plainly visible.

THE PEACE TREATY

Since the surrender of Cornwallis at Yorktown, everyone realized that the War was practically over. General Howe and Clinton toyed with the idea of making a new effort with headquarters in

Delaware, but abandoned the plan on instructions from England.[16] In celebration of the American victory at Yorktown, the citizens of New Castle "to manifest their joy erected a flag-pole near the state-house, on which were hoisted the American continental colours a little above those of the British." Thirteen platoons of muskets were fired, the town illuminated, and toasts drunk. When the British flag blew down, it was regarded as a happy omen.[17] Gayer festivities took place at New Castle in April, 1783, when the news arrived in America that negotiations for peace were completed. Drink and food to the amount of £251 were consumed, for part of which sum a tavern keeper later had to petition the legislature.[18] Though the War had ended, the problem of what to do with exiled loyalists who might desire to come back to their former homes remained.

THE TREATMENT OF RETURNING LOYALISTS

Patriots had no intention of sharing the fruits of their glorious victory with their hated opponents. If departed loyalists returned, they would receive an unpleasant reception. "This day [June 18] a brig arrived here from New York," wrote a correspondent of the *Pennsylvania Packet* from Wilmington in 1783, "the master's name Thomas Rawlings (formerly a resident of this state) and in the early part of the late war, abandoned his country in the time of her distress, and joined, aided and abetted the British forces— Upon Rawlings' coming on shore, and notice thereof being given to the magistrates, they sent for him and very judiciously ordered him to depart the state by 9 o'clock the next morning."[19] At Dover on June 12, the President of Delaware reviewed the Fifth Delaware Regiment commanded by Colonel Gibbs. Afterwards in convention its members resolved that until the Assembly acted upon the fifth article of the peace treaty "we will not suffer refugees from this or any of the United States to reside within the district of this regiment. And if there should be found lurking among us, any of the miscreants, whom we are obliged to consider as worse than robbers or even common murderers,—*as men hardened in utter disaffection to their native country,* we do pledge ourselves by the sacred ties of honour, to be united and stand by each other, in expelling them from among us, by those powers which nature has given us." An association of officers was formed to see that all returned loyalists departed on two days' notice.[20] The Whigs of Sussex County had held a similar meeting for the same purpose on May 16. Sergeants of militia companies were to keep strict watch that no such persons returned. If the loyalists persisted in staying after the issuing of a warning, the sergeants were to summon six officers from the various regiments to carry out the command. The citizens of Lewes had already refused to sell corn to the master of a refugee boat.[21]

These associations overacted their part in the next few elections by attempting to do the impossible of preventing the Tories from voting. Violence characterized the election of October, 1783, in Kent and Sussex Counties. At one polling place in Kent County the ballot box had been removed by an armed band; at another a "violent attack upon the Constitution and Laws of the County" occurred.[22] In Sussex County "a number of officers and Soldiers lately in the Pay of the Continent, and also one of the Inspectors and his Clerk appeared at the place of holding the General Election with Swords, Bayonets and Clubs and uttered many menacing Speeches to terrify the Electors, and actually committed a most violent and outrageous Riot in beating and abusing several persons." Many citizens who had signed the oath of allegiance were denied the franchise privilege.[23] In the election of October, 1787, four petitions from 121 residents of Sussex County complained that "the Freedom of the late general Election for the said County was obstructed by an armed Body of about two hundred Men, known by the Name of Associators."[24] Voters had been beaten, wounded, and maimed. Naturally, such an abnormal state of affairs did not exist for long, and conditions were speedily rectified.

Before the peace treaty had been signed, loyalists had returned to Delaware and been allowed to stay. Luke Shields, a pilot from Lewes named in the excepted list of 1778, had served on a British ship until it had been captured by the French. For his valuable services to his new masters, Robert Morris and the Duke de la Luzerne petitioned the legislature to permit his return. In 1782, the body graciously granted the boom, but Shields was stopped on his entrance into Sussex County and forced to give security for his appearance in the Court of Oyer and Terminer on a charge of high treason. The Assembly then removed his name from the excepted list.[25] Samuel Davis, another pilot, had a similar experience. According to his story, he had been captured by the British and taken to New York where he had been compelled to guide a refugee boat. Finally, he was captured and confined in the

Philadelphia jail. On his release, though he had gone to New York against his will, the pilots at Lewes would not allow him to earn a living; he therefore petitioned the legislature for some sort of pardon.[26] James McKeever, of Wilmington, a resident of Baltimore in 1783, also had a long-winded tale of how he had been seized and held by the British until he escaped. Because of reports spread of his Toryism by William Paul of Philadelphia, he did not dare come home; so he published a true account in a Maryland newspaper to explain the circumstances.[27] In October, 1783, the Rev. Mr. Addison of Prince George's County, Maryland, visited Delaware in an effort to recover some of his lost property.[28] Jacob Smith of Brandywine Hundred sailed to Nova Scotia after the evacuation of New York in 1783, but had returned home by 1785.[29] By 1789 the arch-traitor of them all, Thomas Robinson, had come back to Sussex County to die at the home of his brother, Peter.[30]

Among the Delaware loyalists present in Canada shortly after the signing of the peace treaty were John Watson, John Drake, Joshua Hill, Abraham Wiltbank, Nehemiah Field, Simon Kollock, William Milby, Thomas Robinson, Jacob Smith, Benjamin Galloway, Theodore Maurice, Joseph Burton, and Thomas Gill.[31] The nine men first mentioned above were named in the excepted list of 1778. Joseph Dawson, a trader of Christiana Bridge, and Robert Christie, a lawyer of Wilmington, fled to the British Isles.[32] Of course the great majority of loyalists remained in Delaware. The legislature was inclined to treat the Tories leniently. In 1787 it restored the confiscated property of James Rench of Sussex County, and the heirs of Boaz Manlove and Cheney Clow were encouraged to present petitions in hope of similar redress.[33] At last in 1789 some citizens of Sussex County petitioned for the grant of the right of suffrage.[34] In its next session the Assembly decided to wipe out old wrongs and allowed all Tories full citizenship.[35] Thus ended the story of the Delaware loyalists.

CHAPTER V.

Religion and the Clergy in the Revolution

NO account of the War would be complete without some discussion of the role that religion and the clergy played in the struggle. Scattered over Delaware in about three-score churches in 1775, the clergy had an excellent opportunity to inflence their parishioners powerfully for or against the Revolution from their pulpits. The minister was often the only well-educated man in the village; his prestige was great, and sometimes he conducted a school. Many persons would be affected by the attitude that he might assume. The General Assembly promptly recognized the influence of the clergy in 1777 by forbidding ministers to affirm King or Parliament. Unfortunately, less is known about the part that the congregations which these men served played as a whole, but in general the great majority seem to have followed the guidance of their spiritual leader. Some groups by attachment to England or to the established order were destined to be loyalist, others through tradition, race, or environment became patriot, while one sect on the grounds of religious belief remained pacifist. Sometimes religion was a decisive factor in determining which side of the Revolution one should join.

PRESBYTERIANS

In number of churches and influence the Presbyterians were the strongest sect in Delaware in 1775. Of their 29 churches, more than the combined total of all other denominations, 17 were established in New Castle County, 4 in Kent, and 8 in Sussex.[1] Their preponderance in the northern section of Delaware is largely explained by the presence of numerous Scotch-Irish immigrants, who naturally adhered to this denomination upon their arrival in America.[2] Neither church nor race possessed any special love for

England; both had long stood up for civil rights and liberty. Specific examples from each county will demonstrate how the leaders of the Presbyterians almost uniformly favored independence. Mr. Montgomery, of the town of New Castle, enlisted as a chaplain in the Continental Army.[3] After the Battle of Brandywine, Rev. Dr. Thomas Read assisted Washington's retreat by his knowledge of the countryside. On occasion he marched with the Continental Army. In 1776, with 40 or 50 neighbors, he armed himself and marched to Philadelphia. But the success of the Americans at Princeton and Trenton made it unnecessary for him to enlist.[4] Not only did the son of Rev. John Miller, of Dover, serve in the American army,[5] but the preacher himself urged Caesar Rodney to cross-examine Tories in Kent County closely to discover if any had participated in the Sussex insurrection of 1776.[6] The ingenious plan of Matthew Wilson, of Lewes, to end the Tory menace in 1778 has been described at some length.[7]

Anglican clergymen had an additional incentive in these years for discrediting the Presbyterians. Timoleon observed that the Anglican ministers alarmed their congregations by claiming that "the *Church* was put in imminent danger from a Presbyterian *faction*."[8] "They told their hearers," wrote Thomas McKean in striking confirmation of the statement, "many of whom, especially in Sussex, were illiterate, ignorant, and bigoted, that it was a plan of the Presbyterians to get their religion established; that it originated in New England and was fostered by the Presbyterians in every colony or province."[9] In 1775, Daniel Varnum was brought before the committee of public safety for saying that he would as soon live under a tyrannical King as a tyrannical Presbyterian commonwealth.[10] In a report to the Society for the Propagation of the Gospel, the Rev. Mr. Tingley, Episcopalian rector at Lewes, commented dryly that his parishioners had been faithful to the mother country, "two, or three families excepted, who tho' Churchmen by profession are Presbyterians by trade. These joined with the hot-brained Zealots among the Presbyterians, who have, almost without exception, been fiery advocates for Independence."[11] One could hardly ask for a better confirmation of the patriotism of Presbyterian congregations than such a declaration from a loyalist.

ANGLICAN

In striking contrast is the record of the second strongest sect in Delaware. As uniformly as the Presbyterians supported the rebel side, the Episcopalians backed Great Britian. Of their 12 churches, 4 were in New Castle County, 3 in Kent, and 5 in Sussex.[12] Although the Presbyterians controlled more churches in lower Delaware, Thomas McKean claimed that five-eighths of the population in Kent County and two-thirds in Sussex were Episcopalian.[13] With possibly two exceptions, the representatives sent out by the Society for the Propagation of the Gospel were loyalist. Mr. Ross, of the town of New Castle, escaped the taint. Upon his death in 1782 the principal officials of the government attended his funeral.[14] Probably his patriotism caused complications when his daughter tried to collect his back salary.[15] As early as March, 1775, the Rev. Mr. Reading of Appoquinimink, encountered difficulties in performing his duties and remaining loyal to his most gracious Sovereign.[16] A year later his position was more precarious. *"No more passive obedience and non resistance* has been scribbled with a pencil on my Church door. It was urged as a just cause of complaint against one of the Captains of the Militia that he lugged his company to Church on the day of a public fast *to hear that old wretch* (meaning myself) *preach, who was always an enemy to the present* measures."[17] On July 28, 1776, he was forced to close his church for six weeks, as he "could not read the Liturgy agreeably to the prescribed form without offending against our Government and incurring the resentment of the people," and it was not reopened.[18]

Rev. Samuel Magaw, of Dover, assumed a more moderate position. Like other Episcopalian ministers, he at first reported that his flock held a strong attachment for the mother country.[19] But later he preached two sermons not unfriendly to the Revolution, one dedicated to Caesar Rodney.[20] Francis Asbury thought so much of this "kind, sensible, friendly minister" that he tried to convert him.[21] In performing his duties Mr. Magaw does not seem to have been molested, and even after his transfer to St. Paul's Church returned on occasion to deliver a sermon.[22] In 1780 he accompanied Caesar Rodney on the road to services at Appoquinimink.[23] In January, 1781, he preached at Banit's [sic] Chapel, where he was assisted in the administration of the Lord's Supper by Mr. Thorne.[24]

As early as September, 1775, the Rev. Sydenham Thorne with charges in both Kent and Sussex Counties was summoned before the Kent County Committee of Correspondence for refusing to observe July 20 as a day of fasting as requested by the Continental

Congress and for inciting others to remain loyal to Great Britain, though the action taken by the Committee is unknown.[25] In October, 1778, he reported to the Society for the Propagation of the Gospel that he could "not recollect a single member belonging to either of his congregations who hath taken an active part against the Government."[26] After the legislative act of 1777 he was unable to preach for a short period, but in 1782 he reported that it had been almost two years since he had resumed his duties. Since Mr. Magaw's departure he had also officiated at the Dover Church, and a new building at St. John's Town was being erected under his direction.[27]

When militia and Continental troops were stationed in Sussex County, they mainly attended the Presbyterian Church at Lewes, and an unusual number of marriages between the soldiers and fair maidens of the neighborhood are noted in the records.[28] On the other hand, several members of the Vestry Board of Mr. Tingley's Episcopalian Church at Lewes were prominent loyalists, including Thomas Robinson, and one of the wardens, Luke Shields, was named in the excepted list.[29] Since almost all Episcopalian ministers were loyalists, largely because of their English connections, it is amazing that the legislature accorded the delinquents such mild treatment. The act of 1777 was only temporarily enforced. During the early years of the Revolution, Mr. Magaw at Dover and Mr. Ross at New Castle seem to have been undisturbed. Mr. Tingley kept his church open throughout the struggle, though he was not always allowed to conduct the services personally. By 1780 Mr. Thorne, of Kent and Sussex Counties, had begun to preach again. In large part congregations followed the clergy in being loyalist.

QUAKERS

Because they remained true to their teachings during the War, the Quakers were unable to aid either side. As a result, they suffered taunts and insults, and under protest they paid taxes and military fines which supported a warring government. By 1775 the Quakers had established 12 churches in Delaware.[30] In reviewing their stand towards the War in 1785, the Quakers of Duck Creek Meeting said: "And whereas our Ancient Testimony being against joining in with, pulling down, or setting up of Governments, many of us found ourselves religiously bound in Support of this Testimony, from having anything to do with the Government in the unsettled state thereof during the late Commotions, even to use it on any Occasion; whereby some were sufferers illegally, and sought no Remedy therefor, this Restraint extended to refuse active Compliance to contribute to the Support thereof by payment of Taxes demanded for that Purpose."[31]

Typical of the treatment accorded the Friends by the Whigs were the cases of John Cowgill and Robert Holliday, of Kent County, in 1775. For refusing to accept Continental money, since it might aid the American army, Cowgill was brought before the committee of public safety and later hauled through the streets of Dover amidst the cries of the populace. Holliday in a letter printed in a Philadelphia newspaper declared that nine out of ten in his county would rally around the King's standard if it were raised; the committee of public safety forced him to retract his rash statement.[32] Elizabeth Shipley, Quaker exhorter, foresaw a glorious American victory on her deathbed in 1778.[33]

During the British invasion the Quakers in New Castle County were badly treated by both sides; members of the Wilmington Monthly Meeting filed the following report at the quarterly session in Chester:[34]

> On the 27th of the 8th mo. 1777 Friends Meeting House in Wilmington was forcibly taken of by soldiers belonging to the American Army (who Lay in the Neighborhood of of this Town) and the 28th being our week Day Meeting Friends made Demand of it to hold Meeting in, Some of the officers promised we Should have it but they Did not perform but kept possession, and Friends, not being easy to be Deprived of the privilege of Meeting in their own House Endeavour'd to meet as near it as conveniency would admitt; the meeting was held under a Shady Tree in the graveyard to a good degree of Satisfaction and our thus holding it appeared to be of use for altho the Same as well as other Companies kept possession of it for some time yet at Friends request way was made So that we had some part of the House to meet in afterward, also in the 9th mo. 1777 the British army took possession of our Town and made a garrison of it for their Sick and wounded when Friends war [sic] much oppressed with having Sick and wounded officers with their attendance put into their families where they Remained about for weeks before they were Removed.— and the winter following a Division of the American Army wintered here and Friends ware much oppressed with having both officers and Soldiers placed in their Families.

The members of the meeting estimated that damage amounting to thousands of pounds had been done their property. Throughout the War the Quakers were forced to pay numerous militia fines and war taxes, but they remained faithful to their religious tenets.

METHODISTS

Other denominations had insignificant followings in Delaware. The minister of the one Baptist Church, the Rev. Morgan Edwards, retraced loyalist sentiments in 1775.[35] After this humiliation he retired from preaching permanently. His sons divided in allegiance, one serving in the British Army, the other in the American.[36] Until after the signing of the peace treaty, the Methodists had no church in Delaware, but their ministers carried the Gospel to every nook and corner in the State. In 1782, Mr. Tingley complained that for the past three years he had had "to encounter with the enthusiastic notions of swarms of ignorant Methodists & Anabaptists, whose absurdities seem to him to have direct tendency to overturn all order & decency in the Church, as the wretched principles of those who call themselves Whigs (a softer name for Rebels!) have to overturn the State."[37] Since John Wesley strongly backed Great Britain, his representatives in America were often unjustly suspected of Toryism, and frequently they were maltreated. When Methodist ministers were expelled from Maryland, they found a friendly refuge in Delaware.

Ministers of all denominations opposed them. The Anglican rector at Lewes told his followers it was unlikely that they would "be converted by thunder and lightening," while his Presbyterian colleague, who usually disagreed with him on all subjects, said that the Methodist missionaries "could not be sent and ordained of God—that we [Methodists] must be sent of the devil."[38] The *Journal* of Francis Asbury reveals that he was profoundly depressed during his stay at the home of Judge Thomas White in Kent County in March, 1778: "three thousand miles from home—my friends have left me—I am considered by some as an enemy of the country—every day liable to be seized by violence, and abused."[39] Just before the Battle of Brandywine, Caesar Rodney wrote Washington that the Methodists in western Kent County were raising an insurrection, but nothing else is heard of it.[40] Cheney Clow's rebellion was led by a "back-sliding Methodist," though only two of his followers were members of that faith.[41] As a sequel to this incident, when Rev. Freeborn Garrettson entered Dover, "a proverb for wickedness," on September 12, 1778, the first time that a Methodist minister had ever preached there, he had scarcely alighted from his horse before he was surrounded by a raging mob; "some said, he is a good man, others said, any, he deceived the people—and I was also accused of being a friend to King George. They cried, 'He is one of Clowe's men—hang him—hang him!'" Fortunately, some leading citizens intervened, and he was allowed to proceed.[42] In 1780 Garrettson was arrested on suspicion of Toryism in Dorchester County, Maryland, but was released on £20,000 bond, while he procured a certificate of character from the Executive Council in Delaware. Judge White and Caesar Rodney gladly signed such a paper.[43] The lot of the Methodists was a hard one, but a martyr complex increased their zeal in the face of obstacles. Asbury's hope that "Delaware will become as the garden of the Lord filled with plants of his own planting" became a reality before his death.[44] The attitude of other denominations towards the War is unimportant.

CHAPTER VI.

Conclusions

DIVISION OF THE LOYALISTS INTO CLASSES

*I*N a famous essay Moses Colt Tyler divided the loyalists into five classes.[1] Delaware's contribution to their number may well be considered under these headings. The first class consisted of government officials, their families, and social connections. Since Delaware was not a royal colony and a proprietorship of the weakest type, it contained few such persons. There is, however, one excellent illustration, an official who held the most important crown offices in the province. After 24 years of service and in spite of solicitations to remain, Theodore Maurice, of the town of New Castle, found it necessary to leave his beloved adopted home in June, 1778, despairing of seeing the King's government restored. In 1785 he petitioned His Majesty for redress, for "at the Dissolution of the King's Authority there, he was possessed of the first, the most considerable, and most lucrative offices in that Government, being Prothonotary of the Common Pleas for the County of New Castle, Register for the Probate of Wills, Comptroller of Customs at New Castle town." His salary had averaged £780.[2] Jacob Moore, King's attorney and later a prominent loyalist of Sussex County, resigned his office in 1776.[3] The incident of tax-collector Byrnes who was severely maltreated by a bunch of Whigs with a sense of humor has been commented upon.[4]

In the second class are colonial politicians, who took a selfish view of the dispute for profit's sake. As far as the available records show, Delaware had no representatives in this division. The Crown controlled few offices for distribution among native Americans within the State. A third group include capitalists, commercial interests, and owners of large estates. Thomas Robinson, whose property sold for £34,000, and Joshua Hill, whose

51

possessions brought £5,000, are excellent illustrations of this type.[5] Joshua North was probably the wealthiest loyalist in New Castle County. Jonathan Rumford, a Wilmington merchant of considerable means, got in trouble with the Whigs over the sale of some grain. In 1782, a mob plundered his home; in the excitement his skull was fractured, and he became an invalid for life.[6] The moderate George Read and John Dickinson might also be put in this category. A well-informed writer in the *Sunday Star* claims that Read was at first lukewarm in his support of the War for economic reasons.[7] Dickinson, reputedly the richest man in Delaware, also held back for a time from complete independence.[8]

A fourth group consisted of the professional classes: clergymen, lawyers, teachers, and physicians. The clergy have been considered at great length; as a whole, only the Anglican ministers opposed separation. Among the prominent loyalist lawyers were Charles Gordon, of St. George's Hundred, named in the excepted list, Jacob Moore, and Robert Christie. If one had to qualify as a lawyer before serving on the bench, the list could be considerably extended. George Read and John Dickinson practiced law. Rev. Daniel Currie is an excellent illustration of a loyalist teacher. At first he was attached to the academy at Newark, but when it closed at the beginning of the Revolution, he moved to Dover, where he received £150 for conducting a grammar school and services in Mispillion parish. In 1778 he joined the British in Philadelphia.[9] Among the "practitioners of physic" named in the excepted list are John Watson, Isaac Atwood, and James Rench. Watson was as much a druggist as a doctor; he claimed to have cleared £1,000 annually from his business at New Castle in the years previous to the Revolution, though Thomas Robinson disputed the figure. When Howe visited Delaware, Watson joined his army.[10] Dr. Rench's property was restored to him in 1787.[11]

Many people, wrote Tyler, were loyalists because they were plain conservatives, a group found in every state of society. The great majority of the Delaware loyalists belong to this class, and in environment, one discovers the clue to their conservatism. Delaware was peculiarly isolated from other provinces by geography. There were few schools, few travellers over the bad roads, no newspaper. The mass of the inhabitants were small farmers. Uneducated, uninformed as to what was taking place in the outside world, and poor, they naturally cherished tradition and the established order. Only northern New Castle County escaped the curse of conservatism. Francis Asbury was deeply discouraged by the indifference of Delawareans in the lower sections to their salvation; "for ignorance of God and religion," he recorded in his *Journal* in 1778, "the wilds and swamps of Delaware exceed most parts of America with which I have had any acquaintance."[12] John Dickinson in 1783 classified the Tories remaining in Delaware as "a poor ignorant sett, and, in a political consideration, totally contemptible."[13] Thus, it was extremely easy for preachers, like Tingley and Thorne, and political leaders, such as Robinson and Clarke, to shape the thoughts of their followers. These people—the shallopmen, mariners, husbandmen, tailors, combmakers named in the excepted list of 1778 and the obscure persons who participated in the various insurrections—formed the bulk of the loyalists in Delaware. They were the "cat-paws" manipulated by well-nigh invisible leaders whom the Rev. Mr. Wilson despaired of apprehending. General conservatism is the great underlying factor explaining the rise of the loyalists in Delaware.

Special reasons also operated to produce many Tories. British ships frequented the coasts and tempted the inhabitants to trade at advantageous prices. The great center for such transactions was the Nanticoke River, but all the creeks—Duck, Mispillion, Cedar, Broad—were infested with Tories. During the British invasion residents in New Castle County did not scruple to join in the trade. In the nearby counties of Maryland was a like body of people, from similar reasons as loyalist as their Delaware neighbors, and an interchange of trade and information encouraged rebellion, much to the alarm of Maryland officials. If the inhabitants trafficked with the British or engaged in insurrection, it was unlikely that they would be apprehended by the inefficient militia. If they were caught, Tory judges and juries seldom convicted them; it was sufficient to post a bond. A lenient legislature leaned backward to avoid punishing offenders. Occasionally, the ruthlessness of the militia aroused the ire of the inhabitants, and loyalists fanned the flames into insurrection. Beneath these special reasons is the conservatism of the inhabitants.

WHY THE LOYALISTS FAILED

John Adams in 1780 observed that there were "in this little State, from various causes, more tories in proportion, than in any other."[14] If the loyalists even to a lesser degree approximated the number estimated by Adams, it might be wondered why they did not overrun the State and government more than they are accused of doing. Two factors explain this phenomenon: the superior organization of the Whigs and the influence of agencies outside of Delaware. Following the example set in other colonies, the Whigs in the three lower counties quickly established committees of public safety. In 1775 these bodies were used to punish conservatives for rash statements or to enforce the non-importation agreements, but beginning in the spring of 1776, they had another purpose: to see that no one stood in the path of complete separation. During the discussion over the recommendation of Congress that the colonies set up independent governments, the committees for the first time became important. "When the Question was first Agitated in the committees," wrote Allen McLane about the stirring events in May and June, 1776, "a Considerable Majority was Opposed to the measure, the few whigs (and very few indeed), became Desperate Dreaded the Consequence of being Conquered and treated as Rebels. Attacked the Disaffected with Tar and Feathers, Rotten Eggs &c &c. and succeeded in silencing the Disafected and then filling these Committees with men Determined to be free."[15] Timoleon confirms the picturesque account.[16] Using such methods, the Whigs were able to destroy a counter-petition of the conservatives, have a constitutional convention called, and even squelch the resulting insurrection in Sussex County with the aid of some Continental forces. But the moderates dominated the convention and elected the first legislature; numbers were more important than organization. The inefficiency of the chosen representatives, the revulsion of feeling after the British invasion, and the requirement that voters take an oath of allegiance finally resulted in the meeting of an Assembly, largely Whig, in March, 1778; riots in Sussex County had prevented the gathering of a full legislature earlier. During this session the passage of stricter allegiance laws enabled the whigs to control the government until after 1783. The courts and legislature now took over the work of the committees of public safety in curbing the disaffected, but the committees had laid the foundation for the Whig dominance. The Tories, pushed out of political life, lacking capable leaders, and harassed by committees and militia, could not compete with the superior organization of their opponents.

One reason for the disaffected being kept in some sort of order was the constant interference of outside agencies in the State.

Speaking of the faithfulness of Theodore Maurice to the English cause, Joseph Galloway testified that it was possible for this New Castle loyalist to remain in Delaware as late as June, 1778, "without trimming—as they were moderate People in the Delaware Government—There was throughout the War a Majority in favor of retaining their Allegiance, but it was a small Govt. surrounded by larger ones and incapable of acting of itself."[17] Thus, he suggests that external forces might have had something to do with checking Tory activities. At various times the governments of Pennsylvania and Maryland and the Continental Congress intervened. Pennsylvania stationed Henry Fisher as a lookout scout at Lewes to report on incoming vessels, and it kept an anxious eye on Tory developments within the boundaries of its near neighbor. Its committee of public safety was constantly applied to for guidance. The Maryland authorities were alarmed by the encouragement that their disaffected received from Delaware and frequently informed Congress of Tory plots originating in Sussex before the government of the three lower counties had heard of the schemes. On several occasions Congress felt impelled to send troops to Delaware. In 1776 soldiers under Colonel Miles came to Lewes to investigate an insurrection in Sussex County; in 1777 Colonel Richardson, of the Maryland militia, was busy Tory-catching in the same locality. After the British had left the State, General Smallwood was stationed in Wilmington to prevent the enemy from drawing supplies from Delaware. Undoubtedly, the certainty that one of these three agencies would hop into a disaffected area with ample forces discouraged rebellion. The superior organization of the Whigs in committee prepared the way for their later control of the government, and the soldiers of other states and of Congress helped suppress insurrections that the local militia could not begin to cope with. Thus, the reasons that the Tories did not dominate the legislature and overrun the State in a more serious fashion are explained.

THE LOYALISTS CONSIDERED BY COUNTIES

Some sections of Delaware contained more loyalists than others. Undisputedly, the most patriotic county was New Castle. Perhaps its Scotch-Irish population, its strong Presbyterian Church, and its closeness to the outside world throw light on the phenomenon. Yet after the Battle of Brandywine an amazing number of disaffected appeared. In Kent County were more loyalists than it is commonly supposed. As early as February, 1775, a resident maintained that nine out of ten citizens were still faithful to the mother country, though of course a declaration at this date means little.[18] In May, 1776, John Haslet thought that Congress would have to disarm the lower counties to see its resolve for the establishment of independent governments carried out in Delaware.[19] Thomas McKean in February, 1778, placed Kent and Sussex Counties in the same category as disaffected.[20] The two Anglican ministers within its borders considered their followers firmly attached to Great Britain.[21] Caesar Rodney was continually engaged in hunting down Tories, especially along the Duck, Murderkill, and Mispillion Creeks. In the summer of 1777 Chief Justice Killen feared either a Tory or British attack on Dover, since the disaffected were anxious to release some of Rodney's prisoners.[22] One serious disturbance, Cheney Clow's rebellion, and two minor "insurrections"—one at Dover in the spring of 1776 and another at Jordan's Island in March, 1778—took place.

The most serious Tory outbreaks occurred in Sussex County. Both Assembly and Congress officially declared that the bulk of its inhabitants were loyalist.[23] An Englishman, who had escaped from Baltimore jail in the early part of 1776, thought that the residents in the countryside for sixty or eighty miles around Lewes were well disposed towards Great Britain.[24] Loyalists and patriots were in the proportion of six to one, said some Whigs of Broad Creek in July, 1776.[25] Colonel Richardson, of the Maryland militia, who was stationed in Sussex County during the summer of 1777, believed that the majority of the population retained their fondness for His Majesty's Government.[26] The Anglican rector at Lewes praised his flock for their almost united opposition to independence.[27] The Presbyterian minister at Lewes, Rev. Wilson, reckoned four-fifths of the inhabitants Tories.[28] In 1776, 1500 citizens participated in an insurrection, and in a second in 1780, 400.[29] Using such observations as the basis for an opinion, one might estimate that one-fifth of the population in New Castle County, one-half in Kent, and four-fifths in Sussex were loyalist, or approximately half of the inhabitants of the State.

DELAWARE A LOYALIST STATE

As a whole, Delaware was commonly considered a Tory province. At one time or another, Whigs, such as John Adams,[30] Thomas

McKean,[31] Thomas[32] and Caesar Rodney,[33] Mathew Wilson,[34] John Haslet,[35] and Timoleon[36] declared that the majority of the people were disaffected. They agree with Anglican ministers,[37] British officers,[38] and exiled Tories[39] about the number of loyalists present in Delaware. In opposition are Rev. Joseph Brown Turner, who, before full records were published, estimated that the Diamond State contained fewer Tories in proportion than any colony south of New England except Virginia, or less than 10,000 in round figures, and Judge Conrad, who by implication suggested that most Delawareans were patriots.[40] A writer for the *Sunday Star* declared that half of the population was loyalist.[41] No one attempted to consider the group represented by pacifists, like the Quakers, and hesitants, who perched on a fence waiting to see whom victory favored. Any opinion as to the number of loyalists is open to criticism, since records are incomplete and historians can always find some evidence to support varying judgments. In agreement with the writer for the *Star,* I state as a personal belief that half of the inhabitants were loyalist. The remainder may be divided into a pacifist and hesitant element representing 20% of the population and a patriotic faction consisting of 30%. In brief, I think that 17,000 Delawareans might be classified as loyalists; 7,000, as hesitants or pacifists; and 12,000, as revolutionists. That the great majority of the inhabitants were opposed to or indifferent to independence, in my opinion, cannot be denied. John Adams' theory that a minority backed the American cause through to a successful finish is demonstrated within a small area.

APPENDIX

Thomas Robinson

The most prominent of the Delaware loyalists from the point of view of influence and possibly wealth was Thomas Robinson, of Sussex County. No other loyalist was so active in politics, commanded so much respect, and instituted such active measures to keep the lower counties faithful to their British allegiance. In many ways he contributed to the staunch loyalism of Sussex County.

In 1775, Robinson was 45 and at the height of his vigor. He owned over 1,000 acres of farmland in Indian River and Rehoboth Hundreds, parts of which he leased, and the remainder he tilled with the aid of eight slaves. He also conducted a prosperous store. His family consisted of his wife, two sons, and two daughters. He was well-educated and a member of the Anglican Church. That his neighbors had confidence in him was shown by his repeated elections to the Assembly. Caesar Rodney and other political leaders found it advisable to consult him frequently about political matters as the acknowledged head of the Sussex delegation. This secure and satisfactory way of life Robinson rejected for duty to his King and exile.

A Committee of Correspondence had been formed in Sussex County on June 20, 1775, and the activities of Robinson as head of the "Church party" demanded instant attention, but it was not until taunts of inefficiency and fear were made that the Committee faced its powerful enemy. But his attempts "openly and boldly to stamp his vile and slavish Ministerial principles upon the weak and unwary, over too many of whom, in the forests of Sussex and Maryland, by means of his office and store, he has indeed too much influence" required that something be done. Had not witnesses testified that he had sold tea, had declared Congress to be "an unconstitutional body of men," and had considered the poor "a pack of fools" to arm against the King? When Robinson was summoned to appear before the body on July 22, he sent word "that he did not, nor could not think of coming before them, unless he could bring forty or fifty armed men with him." Resolving that Robinson was "an enemy to his Country and a contumacious opposer of liberty and the natural rights of mankind," the Committee commanded all persons to break off all dealings and commercial relations with him. In a letter to the *Pennsylvania Journal* in October, Robinson complained that the Committee had exceeded its powers, for only a few members had signed the resolutions. Five of the members of the Committee in a written statement declared the charges to be "without foundation." Robinson was not overawed by the action of the Committee and appears to have emerged the victor.

When Robinson was on his way to a meeting of the Assembly in March, 1776, he was jailed by some militia officers at Dover until his conduct could be investigated. Because his companion, Colonel Jacob Moore, who was also a member of the Assembly, drew his sword and dramatically offered to defend Robinson's life at the risk of his own, he also was held. The members in the Assembly from Kent County urged the immediate release of the two delegates on account of urgent business. After they had expressed regret for their imprudent actions and agreed to allow the legislature to determine their fitness for a seat in the Assembly, they were allowed to proceed to New Castle. A resolution signed by the militia officers at Dover specifically exempted Thomas Rodney from ordering the seizure. Timoleon gives George Read, "tyrant of Delaware," the credit for the failure to prosecute.

Following the recommendation of Congress to establish governments friendly to the idea of separation, the Whigs in June circulated petitions calling a constitutional convention. The Tories immediately circulated a counter-petition, which Robinson claimed that he had composed. The Tories asserted that they obtained 5,000 signatures, and the Whigs, only 300. As John Clark, of Kent County, was on his way to present the Tory document to Congress, he was seized, put in the pillory, and the petition destroyed.

This event, said Robinson, led directly to an insurrection. Under his direction and command, 1500 men assembled near Lewes and requested arms and ammunition from Sir Andrew Snape Hammond, which the commander of the *Roebuck* was forced to refuse in view of his scanty supply. The small garrison at Lewes was blockaded until Congress sent 3,000 militiamen from Pennsylvania under Colonel Miles to disperse the Tories. Along with other leaders placed under bond, Robinson was forced to post two bonds of £2,500 each. The Assembly soon pardoned all the participants.

Shortly afterwards Robinson left Delaware, though the exact date of his departure is unknown. J. F. D. Smith, an escaped British prisoner from Baltimore jail and a refugee in Sussex County, stated that Robinson boarded the *Roebuck* on March 13, 1776. According to Robinson's own statement and legislative record, the date is erroneous. Robinson merely declared that having been charged with furnishing the *Roebuck* with supplies in 1776 and being ordered seized by the Assembly, he fled to the British man-of-war *Preston,* leaving behind his family and property valued at £5,000, later confiscated and sold. The proceedings of the Assembly reveal that Robinson was directed to be imprisoned as "an Enemy to the American cause" in January, 1777, because of a letter written in November to James Garrigen, of New York. One can safely conclude that Robinson escaped between June and December, 1776.

When Howe sailed up the Chesapeake in August, 1777, Robinson aided him in obtaining pilots. Robinson had urged that Howe land him with 500 men at Lewes, where 6,000 men might be recruited on a march up the peninsula to Howe's land place. During the winter Robinson resided in Philadelphia, apparently at the same place as the captured President McKinly. He accompanied Colonel Campbell to Georgia in 1778, and in 1779 Sir Henry Clinton made Captain of Safe Guards at Charlestown, with pay of 5 shillings per day. When the British evacuated New York, Robinson went to Nova Scotia, where he acquired a farm at Wilmot. His two sons were with him, one being a half-pay ensign. In June, 1784, he testified before the Commission sent over from England to acquire information concerning losses of loyalists.

Whether Robinson was the wealthiest Delaware loyalist is a debatable question. He claimed that he had left behind property valued at £5,000 when he left Delaware. Rev. John Patterson, of Kent County, Maryland, asserted that he was "a man of the first property in those parts." Joseph Galloway, who had known Robinson for twenty years, said that he "had greater Influence there (Sussex) than any other." When his property was sold, it brought £34,000. Next in value was the property of Joshua Hill sold for £5,000. Both of these figures seem to have been in inflated Continental currency. In a memorandum to the loyalist commission, Hill valued his property at £8,693 Sterling money and £14,498 Pennsylvania currency. He owned over 2,000 acres of land in Delaware and Maryland, unconfiscated land of an unknown amount in North Carolina, a house on Vine Street in Philadelphia, 17 slaves, 20 horses, 95 oxen, 100 hogs. Nehemiah Field testified that "he was thought the richest man that left that Province." While Robinson undoubtedly had greater influence and more political ability, Hill may have been the wealthier.

Robinson did not remain long in Nova Scotia. Armed with a certificate of bad health from Dr. Samuel Seabury, he returned to the home of his brother, Peter Robinson, later Chief Justice, in Sussex County, where he died by 1789. Delaware's greatest loyalist was no more.

Loyalists Excepted From Pardon
by the Act of June 26, 1778

NEW CASTLE COUNTY

Jacob Derickson, late captain of militia, Brandywine Hundred. He was indicted for frequently selling cattle to the enemy in the winter of 1777-78.

Joshua North, late captain of militia, Brandywine Hundred. Reputedly, he was one of the wealthiest men in Delaware. His wife refused an offer of £3,000 in settlement of claims on her husband's property.

William and John Almond, husbandmen, Brandywine Hundred. They were indicted in the fall of 1777 for selling cattle to the British.

James Welch, yeoman, Brandywine Hundred. His confiscated property was restored to him by the Assembly in private act in February, 1787.

John Watson, practitioner in physic, New Castle. After being mobbed and insulted Watson joined Howe at the Head of the Elk on August 24, 1777, and served as a surgeon in the army. In the spring of 1778 with Thomas Slater, of Newport, he fitted out a galley to capture "some of the most troublesome and inveterate Rebels of their Acquaintance." He claimed to have lost £1,000 a year income from his drug business in addition to property at about that sum. Robinson disputed the size of his income. After the revolution he was in Canada.

Christian Smith, labourer, New Castle Hundred.

—————— Hackett, weaver, New Castle Hundred.

John Drake, innkeeper, New Castle Hundred. On April 1776, John Drake, innkeeper and clerk in the office of the recorder of deeds, sold his belongings and prepared to join the British. Until the day of the Battle of Brandywine he remained at the home of friends. Because he had zealously supported the crown and advised the people to remain faithful to their British allegiance he was forced to leave. Until rheumatism forced his retirement he served as clerk on the *Roebuck, Scorpion,* and *Adamant.* He lost £57 in property. When Mrs. John Watson and his wife tried to board a British vessel off New Castle, they were fired upon. In 1787 he was in Canada.

Isaac Conner, cooper, New Castle Hundred.

John Greenwood, cooper, New Castle Hundred.

Thomas Nodes, cordwainer, New Castle Hundred.

[Isaac] Atwood, practitioner in physic and combmaker, Christiana Hundred. Atwood served as a captain in the King's American Regiment. In 1781 he was detached an appointed to the cavalry in Georgia. In

August, 1783, on Long Island, he was petitioning Carlton for aid.

Isaac Simmons, labourer, Christiana Hundred.

William Buchan, late innkeeper, Wilmington.

[Christopher] Wilson, coppersmith, Wilmington. Apparently, he was a loyalist of some wealth.

Charles Gordon, attorney at law, St. George's Hundred. Congress ordered his seizure along with Judge Thomas White in April, 1778.

Joseph Judson, mariner, Appoquinimink Hundred. He was indicted in November, 1777, for selling cattle to the British.

Abraham Anderson, mariner, Appoquinimink Hundred.

Alexander Forman, tailor, Pencader Hundred.

KENT COUNTY

Cheney Clow, husbandman, Little Creek Hundred. Cheney Clow built a fort in April, 1778, which was raided by militia under Colonel Pope. Later, in 1782, he was captured after considerable shooting during which one of Sheriff's posse was killed. After several respites he was hanged in 1788.

James Barcas, husbandman, Little Creek Hundred. He, with William Burrows and Samuel Hatfield, was indicted for an attempted rebellion on April 15, 1778. On this and other occasions he had assembled large quantities of arms; he had stolen goods and munition from peaceful citizens. On payment of cost of prosecution he was freed in July, 1778.

Stephen Barcus, husbandman, Little Creek Hundred. Apparently, he was indicted for the same offense. On payment of the cost of prosecution he was freed in July, 1778.

William Burrows, husbandman, Little Creek Hundred. He was indicted for the same offense as James Barcas. On payment of the cost of prosecution he was freed in July, 1778.

Presley Allee, husbandman, Duck Creek Hundred. With Simeon vanWinkle he was indicted for meeting with other unknown persons and instigating an insurrection in November, 1777. Upon payment of cost of prosecution he was was freed in July, 1778.

Simeon vanWinkle, saddler, Duck Creek Hundred. He was indicted for the same offense as Presley Allee and freed in July, 1778.

William Wartonby, bricklayer, Duck Creek Hundred.

James Massey, hatter, Duck Creek Hundred.

Abraham Conner, husbandman, Duck Creek Hundred.

Samuel Hatfield, husbandman, Murderkill Hundred. He was indicted for the same offense as James Barcas. Upon payment of the cost of prosecution he was freed in July, 1778.

John Brinckle, shallopman, Dover Hundred. On October 10, 1777, he sold a shipload of corn to the British stationed in the Delaware River. He confessed to carrying on correspondence and trade with the British. Upon payment of the cost of prosecution he was freed in July, 1778.

Samuel Worden, shallopman, Murderkill Hundred.

William Thompson, shallopman, Murderkill Hundred.

SUSSEX COUNTY

Joshua Hill, one of the members of the Assembly. In March, 1778, he was driven from his home by a mob. He owned over 2,000 acres of land and was probably Delaware's wealthiest loyalist. In 1784 he was in Canada

James Rench, practitioner of physic and member of the Assembly. In 1787 his property was returned to him.

Thomas Robinson, Delaware's most prominent loyalist.

Boaz Manlove, member of the Assembly. In January, 1777, he was ordered seized by the Assembly. His property sold for £2,000.

Dorman Lofland, formerly sheriff of Sussex. In 1777 he was assisting Simon Kollock in purchasing cattle with counterfeit Continental money.

Abraham Wiltbank, late lieutenant. His property sold for £689. In 1786 he was in Canada.

Luke Shields, pilot. His property sold for £11. During the Revolution he was captured by the British and forced by them to pilot British vessels. Upon his return to Sussex County in 1783 he was stopped and made to give security for his appearance in court. The Assembly pardoned him.

Samuel Edwards, pilot.

William Rowland, pilot.

Nehemiah Field, pilot. His property sold for £761. In 1786 he was in Canada.

Simon Kollock, Jr., cooper. He purchased cattle in Sussex County with counterfeit Continental money. His property sold for £111.

Solomon Truitt, Jr., yeoman.

William Milby. In February, 1777, the Assembly ordered his removal from Philadelphia jail. William and Zadoc Milby were at Shelbourne, Nova Scotia, in 1783 and had received grants of land. By their loyalty to the British cause they lost £3,000.

Notes

CHAPTER I.

THE SETTING FOR THE REVOLUTION

1. Rev. Joseph Brown Turner, "Cheney Clow's Rebellion," *Papers of the Historical Society of Delaware,* LVII, 3, 4.
2. Henry C. Conrad, *History of the State of Delaware* (Wilmington, 1908), I, 151, 152.
3. For example, participators in Cheney Clow's rebellion and the Black Camp insurrection; see George H. Ryden, ed., *Letters to and from Caesar Rodney, 1756-1784* (Philadelphia, 1933), 263. C. Rodney to H. Laurens, Dover, April 24, 1778. See also, D. Hall to (?), Lewes, Dec. 3, 1780 (Paper in State Archives). "Having recruited a number of the persons concerned in the late insurrection renders it necessary to make application to you for money to pay them their Bounty . . . " Thirty-six insurrectionists were enlisted at that time; see D. Hall to C. Rodney, Lewes, Dec. 9, 1780, Rodney, *Letters,* 390.
4. Charles Francis Adams, ed., *The Works of John Adams* (Boston, 1850-1856), X, 277. "Official View," Oct. 9, 1780.
5. *Ibid.,* X, 81. T. McKean to J. Adams, Philadelphia, Nov. 15, 1813.
6. Rodney, *Letters, passim.*
7. *The American Loyalists* (Audit Office Transcripts in the New York Public Library), XXXVII, 425-428.
8. B. F. Stevens, *Facsimiles of Manuscripts in European Archives Relating to America, 1773-1783* (n.p., n.d.), XXIV, No. 2068. Ambrose Serle to the Earl of Dartmouth, Off the Coast of New Castle, Oct. 28, 1777.
9. Historical Manuscripts Commission, *Report on the Manuscripts of Mrs. Stopford-Sackville* (London, 1910), II, 218. Unsigned memorandum in the handwriting of Lord George Germain, 1781 (?).
10. Stella H. Sutherland, *Population Distribution in Colonial America* (New York, 1936), 135
11. "Report of the Committee on Linguistic and National Stocks in the Population of the United States," *Annual Report of the American Historical Association for the year 1931* (Washington, 1932), 307. This study says that in 1790 60% of the population in Delaware was of English descent, while only 6.3% of the inhabitants looked to "Ulster Ireland" for a home.
12. *Works of John Adams,* X, 81.
13. Elizabeth Waterston, *Churches in Delaware during the Revolution* (Wilmington, 1925), III.
14. *Works of John Adams,* X, 81.
15. Waterston, *Churches in Delaware,* III.
16. Reginald Harris, *Charles Inglis: Missionary, Loyalist, Bishop* (Toranto, 1937), 57.
17. James Tilton, "Queries," *The American Museum,* V (April, 1789), 381. "It is a prevailing opinion in Delaware that we have the largest and most perfect manufacture of flour, within a like piece of ground, known in the world."
18. Anna T. Lincoln, *Wilmington, Delaware: Three Centuries Under Four Flags* (Rutland, Vt., 1937), 101.
19. Louis Philippe Ségur, *Memoirs and Recollections of Count Ségur* (Boston, 1825), I, 261.

20. Francis Asbury, *Journal of Rev. Francis Asbury* (New York, 1852), I, *passim*.
21. Lyman P. Powell, *History of Education in Delaware* (Washington, 1896), 47, 54.
22. Ségur, *Memoirs*, I, 258.
23. Tilton, "Queries," *The American Museum*, V, 382.
24. General references for this paragraph: J. Thomas Scharf, *History of Delaware* (Philadelphia, 1888), I, 185-220; Conrad, *History*, I, 88-99.
25. Scharf, *History*, I, 186a.
26. *Delaware Archives* (Wilmington, 1919), II, 985. For example, Thomas Robinson, Boaz Manlove, Jacob Moore.
27. *Ibid.*, III, 1420. A. McLane to C. A. Rodney, Wilmington, April 20, 1818.
28. Timoleon (Dr. James Tilton (?) pseud.), *The Biographical History of Dionysius, Tyrant of Delaware* (Philadelphia, 1788), 16-20.
29. Rodney, *Letters*, 74. C Rodney to T. Rodney, Philadelphia, May 1, 1776.
30. Claude Halstead Van Tyne, *The Loyalists in the American Revolution* (New York, 1902), 192.
31. Alexander Fraser, ed., *Second Report of the Bureau of Archives* (Toranto, 1905), I, 519, 520.
32. Peter Force, ed., *American Archives* (Fourth Series) (Washington, 1853), III, 56, 57.
33. *Ibid.*, III, 218, 219; *Pennsylvania Packet*, August 28, 1775. Scharf records incorrectly that the name was Peter *Cahoon;* Scharf, *History*, I, 224.
34. Scharf, *History*, I, 224.
35. *Ibid.*, I, 224.
36. H. Niles, *Principles and Acts of the Revolution* (Baltimore, 1822), 258.
37. *Pennsylvania Ledger*, February 7, 1775; *American Archives* (Fourth Series), I, 1231.
38. *Pennsylvania Journal*, February 22, 1775; *American Archives* (Fourth Series), I, 1231.
39. Report of the Duck Creek Monthly Meeting, July 23, 1775 (Box 17 ms., Friends Historical Society, Arch St., Philadelphia).
40. *Pennsylvania Journal*, March 22, 1775.
41. *Delaware Historical Society Letters* (copies), XI, Case of Joseph Parsons.
42. *Book of the Proceedings and Transactions of the Committee of Correspondence for Kent County* (Ms. in Del. Historical Society Library), Sept. 7, 1775, 31.
43. *Ibid.*, Sept. 11, 1775, 32-35.
44. *Pennsylvania Journal*, Nov. 29, 1775; *American Archives* (Fourth Series), III, 1072.
45. James Bowden, *History of the Society of Friends* (London, 1854), II, 307, 308. The proceedings of the Kent County Committee may be found in *American Archives* (Fourth Series), IV, 564.
46. *American Archives* (Fourth Series), II, 1032, 1033.
47. Niles, *Principles*, 242. S. McMasters to J. Tilton, Lewes, Nov. 14, 1775.
48. *Ibid.*, 243. J. Tilton to S. McMasters, Dover (?), Nov. (?), 1775.
49. *Ibid.*, J. Tilton to J. W. (?), Dover, Nov. 26, 1775.
50. *Pennsylvania Journal*, October 4, 1775; *American Archives* (Fourth Series), II, 1682, 1683.
51. *Pennsylvania Journal*, October 17, 1775.
52. *Ibid.*, October 17, 1775.

53. Niles, *Principles,* 261.
54. *Ibid.,* 262.
55. *Delaware Historical Society Letters* (copies), XI, Articles of Concession of Thomas Robinson and Jacob Moore, Esq.
56. *Ibid.,* Light Infantry of Dover to the Assembly.
57. Timoleon, *Dionysius,* 18.
58. William Stevens Perry, ed., *Historical Collections Recollections Relating to the American Colonial Church* (Hartford, 1871), II, 469. Mr. Reading to S. P. G., Appoquinimink, March 15, 1775.
59. *Ibid.,* II, 481, 482. Mr. Reading to S. P. G., Appoquinimink, March 18, 1776.
60. *Ibid.,* II, 485. Mr. Reading to S. P. G., August 25, 1776.

CHAPTER II.

THE REVOLUTION AND THE TORIES
IN THE EARLY YEARS

1. Scharf, *History,* I, 226.
2. *American Archives* (Fourth Series), VI, 809. Deposition of William Barry, June 11, 1776.
3. J. F. D. Smyth, *A Tour in the United States of America* (London, 1784), II, 330.
4. *Ibid.,* II, 331-333.
5. *Ibid.,* II, 340.
6. *American Papers* (Sparks Ms.—Widener Library), I, 109. Peter Rea to My Lord (?), May 25, 1776. The names of the recruits were Robert Griffin, Obediah Griffin, and Clemont Bayly. Rea was among the inhabitants named in the petition to the Assembly who had participated in the Sussex insurrection of June, 1776; like the others, he was pardoned.
7. Rodney, *Letters,* 77. J. Haslet to C. Rodney, Dover, May 13, 1776.
8. *Hammond Papers* (Ms. in Tracy W. McGregor Collection at University of Virginia), volume A. Entry under March 30, 1776. Sir Andrew Snape Hammond was commander of the British vessel *Roebuck* stationed in the Delaware River and Bay during much of the Revolution. His valuable papers contain few references to Delaware.
9. Rodney, *Letters,* 81. C. Rodney to T. Rodney, Philadelphia, May 17, 1776.
10. *Ibid.,* 82. T. Rodney to C. Rodney, Dover, May 19, 1776.
11. *Ibid.,* 84. T. Rodney to C. Rodney, Dover, May 26, 1776.
12. *Ibid.,* 84. T. Rodney to C. Rodney, Dover, May 26, 1776.
13. *Ibid.,* 88. T. Rodney to C. Rodney, Dover, June 2, 1776.
14. *Ibid.,* 87. J. Haslet to C. Rodney (May, 1776).
15. *Ibid.,* 88. J. Haslet to C. Rodney, Longfield, June 5, 1776.
16. Timolein, *Dionysius,* 12, 13.
17. *Ibid.,* 14, 15.
18. *The American Loyalists* (Transcripts), XXXVII, 390. Memorial of Thomas Robinson.
19. *Ibid.,* XXXVII, 390; Timoleon, *Dionysius,* 20.

20. Enoch Anderson, "Personal Recollections of Captain Enoch Anderson," *Papers of the Historical Society of Delaware,* XVI (Wilmington, 1896), 9, 10.
21. Timoleon, *Dionysius,* 21.
22. Anderson, "Recollections," *Papers of the Historical Society of Delaware,* XVI, 10-13.
23. Rodney, *Letters,* 88, 89. J. Haslet to C. Rodney, Longfield, June 5, 1776.
24. *Delaware Archives,* III, 1364, 1365. H. Fisher to Pa. Council of Safety, Lewestown, June 10, 11, 1776.
25. *American Archives* (Fourth Series), VI, 808. D. Hall to President of Congress, Lewes, June 11, 1776.
26. *Ibid.* (Fourth Series), VI, 833. T. McKean to President of Congress, New Castle, June 13, 1776.
27. *Ibid.* (Fourth Series), VI, 833. T. McKean to President of Congress, New Castle, June 13, 1776.
28. Rodney, *Letters,* 90. T. Collins to C. Rodney (?), June 14 (1776).
29. *Ibid.,* 90. T. Collins to C. Rodney (?), June 12 (1776).
30. William P. McMichael, "Diary of Lieutenant James McMichael of the Pennsylvania Line," *Pennsylvania Magazine of History and Biography* (July, 1892), XVI, 130.
31. *The American Loyalists* (Transcripts), XXXVII, 390. Robinson.
32. *Proceedings of the Convention of the Delaware State, 1776* (Wilmington, 1776; reprint, Wilmington, 1927), 35, 36.
33. *Delaware Archives,* III, 1427. W. Polk to J. Cannon, etc. (Lewes), June 10, 1776.
34. *Ibid.,* III, 1380. D. Hall to J. Wiltbank to W. Polk, etc. (Lewes), June 11, 1776.
35. *Delaware Historical Society Letters* (copies), II, Isaac Bradley to (?), Lewes, June 12, 1776.
36. *Delaware Historical Society Letters* (copies), V. J. Wiltbank, etc., to (?), (Lewes), June 12, 1776. Other names may have been signed, but the paper is broken off.
37. *Ibid.,* XI, J. Dagworthy to Col. Rhodes, (Lewes), June 14, 1776. This letter is dated 1775, but its contents could only have happened in 1776. Apparently this letter was later forwarded to C. Rodney; see Rodney, *Letters,* 90. T. Collins to C. Rodney, (Sussex County), June 14, (1776).
38. *American Papers* (Sparks Ms.—Widener Library), I, 108. The diary was kept by Mr. Parker of Maryland; the entry date is June 19, 1776.
39. *Hammond Papers,* Letter Book V, Andrew Snape Hammond to Sir Peter Parker, Commander in Chief, June 24, 1776. "Roebuck at Givins Island in Virginia." See also, *Hammond Papers, Volume B.* Entry under June 24, 1776.
40. *The American Loyalists* (Transcripts), XXXVII, 390, 391.
41. *Cf.,* 12.
42. D. Hall to Committee of Public Safety in Philadelphia, Lewes, June 20, 1776. (C. E. French Collection, Mass. Historical Society.)
43. *American Archives* (Fifth Series), I, 9-11. D. Hall to Congress, Lewes, July 5, 1776; J. Bell, etc., to Congress, July 5, 1776.
44. *Ibid.* (Fifth Series), I, 11. Testimony of Enoch Scudder.
45. Rodney, *Letters,* 96. J. Haslet to C. Rodney, Lewes, July 6, 1776.
46. *Ibid.,* 99. C. Rodney to Captain Carson, Dover, July 22, 1776.
47. *Ibid.,* Instructions to delegates, New Castle, March 22, 1776.

48. Rodney, *Letters*, 92. Instructions on June 15, 1776.
49. *Ibid.*, 95, 96, footnote 3.
50. *Ibid.*, 96. J. Haslet to C. Rodney, Lewes, July 6, 1776.
51. "Caesar Rodney," *Delaware Register* (February, 1838), I, 25, 26.
52. *Proceedings, 1776*, 5, 6.
53. Reed, "Delaware Constitution of 1776," *Delaware Notes* (Sixth Series), 8-21. An excellent discussion of events prior to the meeting of the Constitutional Convention.
54. Rodney, *Letters*, 99. C. Rodney to T. Rodney, Philadelphia, August 3, 1776.
55. *American Archives* (Fifth Series), I, 1057-1059. An Address Delivered August 19, 1776.
56. *Sparks Manuscripts* (Misc. Papers), II, 80, 81. J. Haslet to C. Rodney (October, 1776).
57. Rodney, *Letters*, 104. T. Rodney to C. Rodney, Dover, August 19, 1776.
58. Timoleon, *Dionysius*, 22.
59. Rodney, *Letters*, 105. C. Rodney to T. Rodney, Philadelphia, August 28, 1776.
60. *Proceedings, 1776*, 17-20; for a discussion see Max Farrand, "The Delaware Bill of Rights of 1776, *American Historical Review* (July, 1898), III, 641-649.
61. *Proceedings, 1776*, 26-35; for an excellent account of preliminaries of the constitution and its provisions, see Reed, "Delaware Constitution of 1776," *Delaware Notes* (Sixth Series), 8-36.
62. Scharf, *History*, I, 235, 236.
63. Rodney, *Letters*, 133. J. Haslet to Caesar Rodney, Camp near Mt. Washington, October 5, 1776.
64. *Sparks Ms.* (Misc. Papers), II, 81. (October, 1776?)
65. John Laws had been disarmed during the insurrection; the other Tory remains unknown.
66. *Delaware Archives*, III, 1367. H. Fisher to Pennsylvania Council of Safety, Lewes, October 25, 1776.
67. Timoleon, *Dionysius*, 26, 27.
68. *Hammond Papers*, volume C, entry of December (?), 1776.
69. Edmund C. Burnett, ed., *Letters of Members of the Continental Congress* (Washington, 1926), III, 138. B. Rush to President of Pennsylvania Council of Safety, Philadelphia, November 1, 1776.
70. William T. Read, *Life and Correspondence of George Read* (Philadelphia, 1870), 138. G. Read to R. Morris, New Castle, November 5, 1776.
71. Perry, *Historical Collections*, V, 128. Mr. Magaw to S. P. G., Philadelphia, October 5, 1776.
72. *Sparks Ms.*, II, 84. J. Haslet to C. Rodney, Nov. 12, 1776.
73. *Ibid.*, II, 84. J. Haslet to C. Rodney, Nov. 19, 1776.
74. Read, *Life of Read*, 221, 222. T. Duff to G. Read, Philadelphia, Dec. 19, 1776.
75. See *post*, 23.
76. Read, *Life of Read*, 299. T. McKean to G. Read, York, Feb. 12, 1778.
77. *Sparks Ms.*, II, 84. J. Haslet to C. Rodney, Nov. 12, 1776.
78. Rodney, *Letters*, 178. T. Rodney to C. Rodney, Dover, Feb. 16, 1778.
79. Timoleon, *Dionysius*, 28, 29.
80. *Pennsylvania Packet*, Feb. 11, 1778. Adv. by A. McLane.
81. Rodney, *Letters*, 429. T. Rodney to C. Rodney, Wilmington, Oct. 19, 1781.
82. *Ibid.*, 58. T. Rodney to C. Rodney, Dover, May 10, 1775.

83. *Ibid.*, 298. C. Rodney to J. Dickinson, Dover, April 17, 1779. The names of the judges were T. Tilton, J. Clarke, R. Smith, and T. White.

84. Timoleon, *Dionysius*, 29.

85. See *ante*, 14; *Proceedings, 1776*, 35. William Polk and John Laws. John Wiltbank was chief justice; nothing is known about Isaac Smith.

86. Rodney, *Letters*, 211. W. Richardson to Continental Congress, Sussex County, August 9, 1777.

87. *Ibid.*, 262. C. Rodney to H. Laurens, Dover, April 24, 1776.

88. See *post*, 31.

89. *Works of John Adams*, 82. T. McKean to J. Adams, Philadelphia, Nov. 15, 1813.

90. Read, *Life of Read*, 298. T. McKean to G. Read, York, Feb. 12, 1778.

91. *Delaware Historical Society Letters* (copies), XII, T. Rodney to C. Rodney (?), Dover, May 12, 1777.

92. *Minutes of the Council of the Delaware State* (Wilmington, 1887), 35.

93. *Ibid.*, 87, 88; J. Thomas Scharf, *History of Philadelphia, 1609-1884* (Philadelphia, 1885), 302.

94. *Votes of the House of Assembly, 1777* (Wilmington, 1777), 36.

95. *Ibid.*, 36.

96. *Ibid.*, 36.

97. *Laws of Delaware, 1777* (Wilmington, 1777), 13, 14. This edition may be consulted in the collection of the Philadelphia Library Company. Only the title of the law is in the edition of 1797, since by that time it had become obsolete; see *Laws of Delaware* (New Castle, 1797), II, 595.

98. *Delaware Archives*, III, 1279.

99. *Votes of Assembly, 1777*, 125, 126.

100. *Ibid.*, 129

101. *Ibid.*, 144.

102. *Delaware Archives*, III, 1281, 1282. David Hall, etc., to President of Congress, Lewes, June 24, 1777.

103. *Journal of Continental Congress*, VIII, 527-530. July 3, 1777.

104. Rodney, *Letters*, 199. C. Rodney to T. Collins, Dover, July 23, 1777.

105. *Ibid.*, J. McKinly to C. Rodney, Wilmington, July 10, 1777.

106. *Ibid.*, 195, 196. C. Rodney to J. McKinly, Dover, July 11, 1777.

107. Read, *Life of Read*, 266, 267. W. Killen to G. Read, Dover, August 9, 1777.

108. Rodney, *Letter*, 196. C. Rodney to J. McKinly, Dover, July 11, 1777.

109. *Ibid.*, 196.

110. *Delaware Archives*, III, 1410. J. McKinly to President of Congress, Wilmington, July 28, 1777.

111. *Ibid.*, III, 1410. For the list of prisoners, see *Ibid.*, III, 1331.

112. Read, *Life of Read*, 265. W. Killen to G. Read, Dover, August 9, 1777.

113. *Delaware Archives*, III, 1284. Cases of Isaac Stedham, David Davis, Branson Lofflin, Littleton Lofflin.

114. Read, *Life of Read*, 267. W. Killen to G. Read, Dover, August 9, 1777.

115. Rodney, *Letters*, 210-212. W. Richardson to Continental Congress, Sussex County, August 9, 1777.

116. *Ibid.*, 203, 204. D. Hall and H. Fisher to C. Rodney, August 2, 1777.

117. *The American Loyalists* (Transcripts), XXXVII, 409, 410. Testimony of Joseph Galloway about T. Robinson.
118. *Hammond Papers,* volume C. Entry of July, 1777.

CHAPTER III.

THE CRITICAL PERIOD

1. *The American Loyalists* (Transcripts), XXXVII, 375-377.
2. *Ibid.,* XXXVII, 458.
3. *Ibid.,* XIII, 23.
4. Rodney, *Letters,* 219. C. Rodney to G. Washington, Middletown, Sept. 6, 1777.
5. Scharf, *History,* I, 243-248.
6. T. McKean to S. Patterson, Lancaster, Oct. 7, 1777. (Letter in Pa. Historical Society.)
7. *Delaware Archives,* III, 1308.
8. *Ibid.,* III, 1307.
Petition of Jesper Beeson to Sir Guy Carlton, May 9, 1783, New York.
10. *Laws of Delaware,* II, 637.
11. *Sparks Ms.,* V, 4. G. Read to S. Patterson, New Castle, Dec. 22, 1777.
12. Stevens, *Facsimiles,* XXIV, No. 2608. A. Serle to Earl of Dartmouth, "Off New Castle, October 28, 1777."
13. *Delaware Archives,* III, 1312.
14. Rodney, *Letters,* 250. C. Rodney to W. Smallwood, Dover, Dec. 25, 1777.
15. *Delaware Archives,* III, 1285, 1286. Pressley Allee and Simon vanWinkle attempted to levy war; John Brinckle sold corn to the British.
16. *Ibid.,* III, 1283. Nov. 17, 1777.
17. Rodney, *Letters,* 247. G. Read to C. Rodney, Dover, Dec. 21, 1777.
18. *Ibid.,* 238-240. W. Peery to C. Rodney, Lewes, Oct. 3, 1777.
19. S. Patterson to T. McKean, Jan. 8, 1778. (Wilmington.) (Letter in Pa. Historical Society.)
20. Read, *Life of Read.* T. McKean to G. Read, York, Feb. 12, 1778.
21. Rodney, *Letters.* S. Patterson to C. Rodney, Wilmington, Jan. 10, 1778.
22. Benjamin Ferris, *A History of the Original Settlements on the Delaware* (Wilmington, 1846), 258-260; for the account in the New Jersey newspaper, see *New Jersey Archives,* 2nd series, II (Trenton, 1903), 102.
23. Timoleon, *Dionysius,* 43.
24. Rodney, Letters, 253-254. C. Rodney to T. McKean, Dover, March 9, 1778.
25. *Minutes of the Council,* 200. March 20, 1778.
26. *Ibid.,* 221, 222. April 10, 1778.
27. *Votes of Assembly, 1778* (Ms. in State Archives), 16, 22.
28. *Laws of Delaware* (1778) (Edition may be consulted in Philadelphia Library Company; only the title is in collected laws), 70, 73.
29. *Ibid.* (1778), 75, 76.
30. *Laws of Delaware,* II, 636-638. June 26, 1778.
31. *Votes of Assembly, 1779,* 9.
32. Report of William McClay, commissioner for New Castle County, Jan. 22, 1781. (Legislative papers—1781—in State Archives.)

33. *The American Loyalists (Transcripts)*, XXXVII, 117. Memorial of Rev. J. Boucher and Daniel Dulany Addison.

34. *Laws of Delaware*, II, 894. Feb. 3, 1787. G. Read may possibly have aided Rench in obtaining his property; see Read, *Life of Read*, 312, 314. G. Read to Dr. Rench, New Castle, August 25, 1778.

35. *Votes of Assembly, 1791*, 16. Petition of Mary Train; *Votes of Assembly, 1790*, 25. Petition of Elisha Burrows who married Arrana Clow.

36. *Delaware Papers* (Library of Congress), I, 33. Report of William McClay, Oct. 31, 1778.

37. Report of William McClay, Jan., 1781 (Legislative Papers—1781—in State Archives).

38. Report of Levin Derickson, Dec. 12, 1781 (Legislative Papers—1781—State Archives). A paper from the State Treasurer's Accounts gives the returns of Levin Derickson and William Perry of Sussex County on Dec. 13, 1781, as $67,057.

39. Report of Levin Derickson, Dec. 12, 1781 (Legislative Papers).

40. Court of Oyer and Terminer for Kent County, 1778, 17-25. (Manuscript in State Archives.)

41. *The American Loyalists* (Transcripts), XXXVII, 425-428.

42. Turner, "Cheney Clow's Rebellion," *Papers of the Historical Society*, LVII, 6.

43. Rodney, *Letters*, 259. Colonel Pope to C. Rodney, Grog or Whiskey Town, April 14, 1778.

44. *Ibid.*, C. Rodney to Henry Laurens, Dover, April 24, 1778.

45. Freeborn Garrettson, *The Experience and Travels of Mr. Freeborn Garrettson* (Philadelphia, 1791), 77.

46. Rodney, *Letters*, 263. C. Rodney to H. Laurens, Dover, April 24, 1778.

47. Court of Oyer and Terminer for Kent County, 1782, 38. (Manuscript in State Archives.)

48. *Votes of Assembly, 1790*, 25, 26.

49. Mention should also be made of an account of Clow's rebellion in *The Delaware Register and Farmers' Magazine* (April, 1838), I, 220-226. Turner's article is based mainly on this source. Professor Ryden in Rodney, *Letters,* gives a corrected version on page 263, footnote 1.

50. *Delaware Archives*, III, 1259, 1260. W. Smallwood to W. Atlee, Wilmington, April 4, 1778.

51. Burnett, *Letters of Members of the Continental Congress*, III, Charles Carroll to Governor of Maryland, York, April 21, 1778.

52. William Beatty, "Journal of Captain William Beatty, 1776-1781," *The Maryland Historical Magazine* (June, 1908), III, 112. April 29, 1778.

53. Rodney, *Letters*, 267. C. Rodney to T. McKean, Dover, May 8, 1778.

54. *Delaware Papers* (Library of Congress), I, 6a. May 6, 1778.

55. C. H. B. Turner, ed., *Some Records of Sussex County, Delaware* (Philadelphia, 1909), 238. Rev. S. Thorne to S. P. G., New York, Oct. 5, 1778.

56. *Maryland Archives*, XVI, 57. Council to Col. Simpson, Feb. 10, 1778.

57. *Second Report of Bureau of Archives*, I, 519, 520; *The American Loyalists* (Transcripts), XIII, 5, 6.

58. *Maryland Archives*, XXI 220. Philadelphia, Oct. 20, 1778. A. Wiltbank.

59. Rev. Edward D. Neill, "Matthew Wilson, D.D., of Lewes, Delaware," *Pennsylvania Magazine of History and Biography* (Nov., 1884), VIII, 52, 53.

NOTES

CHAPTER IV.

THE END OF THE REVOLUTION

1. Rodney, *Letters*, 365. 366. J. Jones to C. Rodney, Sussex County, August 10, 1780.
2. *Ibid.*, 367, 368. J. Collins to C. Rodney, Sussex County, August 22, 1780.
3. *Delaware Archives*, III, 1293.
4. *Ibid.*, III, 1289.
5. *Votes of Assembly, 1787*, 52. Payment of fees to Justices Killen and Jones for 37 cases.
6. *Minutes of Council, 1782*, 754.
7. *Delaware Archives, III*, 1302-1304. Seago Potter, William Bevins, Battholomew Johnson, Jacob Johnson, Isaac Downs, Barnet Downs, Moses Stewart, and John Conway.
8. *Ibid.*, 1304, 1305. Petitions to legislature in 1781 and 1782.
9. *Pennsylvania Journal*, Sept. 6, 1780.
10. *Pennsylvania Packet*, August 16, 1781.
11. *Votes of Assembly, 1787*, 52. "To John Smith, for loss of time and expenses while curing of a wound received, 2d September 1781, in assisting to quell an insurrection in Sussex county."
12. *Pennsylvania Packet*, March 7, 1782.
13. *Pennsylvania Journal*, March 1, 1783.
14. T. McDonough to S. Patterson, St. Georges, Feb. 24, 1783. (Library of Congress—VanDyke papers.)
15. *The Maryland Journal and Baltimore Advertiser*, Jan. 21, 1783.
16. *Clinton-Cornwallis Controversy* (London, 1888), II, 180, Germain to Clinton, Oct. 12, 1781. (No author.)
17. *The Freeman's Journal*, Oct. 31, 1781. Philadelphia.
18. *Delaware Archives*, III, 1482-1484.
19. *Pennsylvania Packet*, June 21, 1783.
20. *The Freeman's Journal*, June 25, 1783.
21. *Ibid.*, June 4, 1783.
22. *Delaware Papers* (Library of Congress), II, 60, 61. Ms.
23. *Ibid.*, II, 57, 62, 63.
24. *Votes of Assembly, 1787*, 8.
25. *Delaware Archives*, II, 940, 941.
26. *Ibid.*, II, 905. Petition of Samuel Davis in June, 1781.
27. *The Maryland Journal and Baltimore Advertiser*, July 22, 1783.
28. *The American Loyalists* (Transcripts), XXXVII, 117.
29. Charles William Heathcote, "Diary of Jacob Smith," *Pennsylvania Magazine of History and Biography* (July, 1932), LVI, 264.
30. *The American Loyalists* (Transcripts), XXXVII, 416.
31. *Ibid.*, XIII, XXXVII, *passim*. Many of them testified concerning the property claims of either Thomas Robinson or Joshua Hill. The favorite place of settlement was Nova Scotia.
32. *Ibid.*, XXXVII, 443. Case of Dawson; *American Papers* (Sparks Ms.— Widener Library), II, 26.

33. See *ante*, 33.
34. *Votes of Assembly, 1789*, 8.
35. *Laws of Delaware*, II, 968, 969. Jan. 27, 1790.

CHAPTER V.

RELIGION AND THE CLERGY
IN THE REVOLUTION

1. Waterston, *Churches in Delaware*, 111. This study does not cover the subject adequately.
2. See *ante*, 3.
3. William B. Sprague, *Annals of the American Pulpit* (New York, 1865-1873) (Presbyterians), III, 33.
4. Henry C. Conrad, *Memoir of Rev. Thomas Read, D.D.*, typewritten paper in possession of Dr. Eliott Field of Dover, one of Dr. Read's descendents. See also Rev. Elliot Field, "Old Drawyers," *The Presbyterian*, May 19, 1938, and John Fiske, *The American Revolution* (Boston, 1891), I, 312-314.
5. Samuel Miller, *The Life of Samuel Miller* (Philadelphia, 1869), I, 29, 30.
6. Rodney, *Letters*, 96. J. Miller to C. Rodney, Dover, July 8, 1776.
7. See *ante*, 36.
8. Timoleon, *Dionysius*, 16.
9. *Works of John Adams*, X, 81. T. McKean to J. Adams, Philadelphia, Nov. 15, 1813.
10. See *ante*, 8.
11. Turner, *Some Records*, 239. Mr. Tingley to S. P. G., New York, March 5, 1782.
12. Waterston, *Churches in Delaware*, 111.
13. *Works of John Adams*, X, 81.
14. *Pennsylvania Packet*, April 20, 1782.
15. Joseph Tatlow, etc., to S. P. G., New Castle, May 6, 1784. (Library of Congress—S. P. G. transcripts.)
16. See *ante*,
17. Perry, *Historical Collections*, II, 481, 482. Mr. Reading to S. P. G., Appoquinimink, March 18, 1776.
18. *Ibid.*, II, 485. Mr. Reading to S. P. G., Appoquinimink, August 25, 1776.
19. See *ante*, 9, 10.
20. Scharf, *History*, II, 1055. These sermons may be examined in the collection of the Philadelphia Library Company.
21. Asbury, *Journal*, I, 307.
22. *Ibid.*, I, *passim*. For example, in June and July, 1779; see 312, 313. The exact date of his transfer is unknown.
23. Rodney, *Letters*, 387. C. Rodney to T. Rodney, Dover, Oct. 9, 1780.
24. Asbury, *Journal*, I, 419. Jan. 21, 1781.
25. See *ante*, 7.
26. Turner, *Some Records*, 238. Rev. S. Thorne to S. P. G., New York, Oct. 5, 1778.
27. *Ibid.*, Rev. S. Thorne to S. P. G., New York, Sept. 16, 1782.

28. Minutes of Lewes Presbyterian Church, 1759-1848, *passim*. (Typewritten manuscript in possession of State Archives.) For example, Captain David Hall married Mrs. Hetty (P. 13); Lieutenant Hazzard married Mary Caldwell (P. 15).
29. Minutes of St. Peter's Protestant Episcopal Church, Lewes, Delaware (Typewritten copy in State Archives), 15, 16. Based on election of April, 1774. Loyalists include Jacob Moore, Philip Kollock, and Daniel Nunez.
30. Waterston, *Churches in Delaware,* 111.
31. Report of Duck Creek Monthly Meeting to Quarterly Meeting at Chester, Little Creek, July 23, 1785. Manuscript in Friends' Historical Society, Philadelphia, box 17.
32. *Ante,* 7.
33. *Ante,* 30.
34. Report of Wilmington Monthly Meeting, 1777-1779, to Quarterly Meeting, Box 15. Manuscript in Friends' Historical Society.
35. *Ante,* 6.
36. Sprague, *Annals* (Baptists), VI, 82. In 1775 the Baptists had only one church; by the end of the Revolution, another church or two. Miss Waterston states that John Adams gave credit to the Baptists "for bringing Delaware from the Gulf of Toryism to the platform of patriotism," citing *Works of John Adams,* X, 812. But a careful examination of the work on that and other pages, does not reveal the source of the quotation. If Adams did make the statement, he was giving much credit to its *one* church.
37. Turner, *Some Records,* 241. Rev. Tingley to S. P. G., New York, March 5, 1782.
38. Asbury, *Journal,* I, 327. Sept. 28, 1779.
39. *Ibid.,* I, 267, 268. April 2, 1778. It is usually said that Judge White was seized because of his Methodist connections, but in my opinion this has not been clearly shown; rather he seems to have been jailed for his part in a loyalist plot. See Rodney, *Letters,* 264. T. McKean to C. Rodney, York Town, April 28, 1778.
40. Rodney, *Letters,* 219. C. Rodney to G. Washington, Middletown, Sept. 6, 1777.
41. Garretson, *Travels,* 77. For a fuller account with the claim about the two Methodists, see Dr. Nathan Bangs, *The Life of Rev. Freeborn Garrettson* (New York, 1829), 64.
42. Garrettson, *Travels,* 93, 94.
43. *Maryland Archives,* XLIII (V), 430, 454.
44. Asbury, *Journal,* I, 280. June 13, 1778.

CHAPTER VI.

CONCLUSIONS

1. Moses Coit Tyler, *The Literary History of the American Revolution, 1763-1783* (New York, 1797), I, 301-303.
2. *The American Loyalists* (Transcripts), XXXVII, 419, 420.
3. Scharf, *History,* I, 404.
4. See *ante,* 7.
5. See *ante,* 33.
6. Elizabeth Montgomery, *Reminiscences of Wilmington* (Wilmington, 1872), 148.

7. *Sunday Star*, Dec. 15, 1935. No author. This article may be conveniently consulted in the files of the Wilmington Library.
8. Miller, *Life of Samuel Miller*, I, 70.
9. *The American Loyalists* (Transcripts), XXXVII, 434, 435.
10. *Second Report of Bureau of Archives* (Ontario), I, 1162-1164.
11. See *ante*, 33.
12. Asbury, *Journal*, I, 312.
13. *The Freeman's Journal*, Jan. 29, 1783. Philadelphia. This statement may also be found in the printed collection of his works.
14. *Works of John Adams*, X, 277. "Official View," Oct. 9, 1780.
15. *Delaware Archives*, III, 1420. A. McLane to C. A. Rodney, Wilmington, April 20, 1818.
16. Timoleon, *Dionysius*, 16-20.
17. *The American Loyalists* (Transcripts), XXXVII, 428, 429.
18. *Ante*, 7.
19. *Ante*, 13.
20. *Ante*, 30.
21. *Ante*, 46, 47.
22. *Ante*, 25.
23. *Ante*, 24, 31.
24. *Ante*, 11.
25. *Ante*, 16.
26. *Ante*, 25.
27. *Ante*, 45.
28. *Ante*, 36.
29. *Ante*, 16, 39.
30. *Ante*, 1.
31. *Ante*, 30.
32. *Ante*, 21.
33. Rodney, *Letters*, 263. C. Rodney to H. Laurens, Dover, April 24, 1778. "I am sorry to say, the Suspicions Congress entertains of the disaffection of the people is too well founded . . . " This is as definite a statement as he makes, but he frequently talks of the "alarming scituation" in Kent County where he is pursuing Tories; see *ante*,
34. *Ante*, 36.
35. *Ante*, 20.
36. Timoleon, *Dionysius, passim*. Practically every page written by this prejudiced politician expresses this sentiment.
37. *Ante*, 46.
38. *Ante*, 2.
39. *Ante*, 34.
40. *Ante*, 1.
41. *Sunday Star*, Dec. 15, 1935.